D0061578

Attilia Dorigato

The Glass Museum

Marsilio

Photographic references
Museo Correr Photograph Archive
Andrea Morucchio

Cover
Small shell cruet, flower goblet
and small bottle with lobed body

Translated by
David Graham

Graphic design of the guide
Tapiro, Venice

Images coordinated by the
Musei Civici Veneziani
Studio Camuffo, Venice

First edition: July 2006
ISBN 88-317-9098

www.marsilioeditori.it

Contents

The Murano Glass Museum, canal facade.

The museum and its collections

The Glass Museum was opened in 1861, when the Murano glass works had begun to show signs of recovery after a very critical period of virtual standstill. The political and economic crisis following the fall of the Serenissima Republic (1797) and subsequent foreign rule had led to the close of all the craft activities in Venice for which it had been renowned over the centuries.
The art of glass blowing in particular, which had brought Murano great prestige all around the world, was almost lost between the end of the eighteenth and the beginning of the nineteenth centuries. Apart from some studios producing pearls, or beads, all those specialising in blown glass had been forced to close. This was primarily because, after setting up the Lombard Veneto Kingdom in 1815, Austria had imposed heavy tariffs on imports of the necessary raw materials and on exports of the finished products in order to encourage the introduction of Bohemian glass into Venetian territories.
It was in this climate that the idea of setting up a small historical archive in memory of the island's past was put forward by Abbot Vincenzo Zanetti (1824-1883), a native of Murano who loved his island and cherished its history, and Antonio Colleoni (1811-1855), city councillor and owner of a pharmacy in Murano at San Lorenzo Giustinian.
The documents and deeds from the council and parish archives were soon collected, as were parchments, codices, antique books, engravings, coins and works of art illustrating the island life, along with a small collection of glass. On 7 October 1861 the Murano City Council appointed Zanetti director of the 'Archive and Collection', providing him with spacious premises in the municipal building of the time, the Palazzo Giustinian.
The glass collection expanded considerably, initially with the few purchases the institution could manage, but mainly by private donations, thanks to the enterprise and persuasive skills of Abbot Zanetti, thus outgrowing the archive and requiring more space where the evidence of the island's past activity could be admired.
In the meantime, the Council delegation had asked those studios that had recently begun making blown glass again, such as F.lli Toso, which opened its doors in 1854, to send the museum some samples of their production so that modern works could be presented alongside those of the past to confirm Murano's vitality.

In the 1860s the institution became a driving force of ideas and stimuli for the new manufacturers. In 1862 a school was attached to the museum. Glass-makers attended this on Sundays, studying not only

design but also the techniques used to produce the examples from the past. Some years later, in 1864 and 1869, the museum organised the First and Second Glass Exhibitions, which were a big incentive for the glass-makers. Finally, in 1867, the glass art periodical *La Voce di Murano* was launched, with the aim of presenting the progress and innovations made by the glass works in those years.
The museum became part of the Musei Civici Veneziani following the closure of the Murano City Council in 1923 and its annexation to the Venice City Council. The glass collections in the Museo Correr were subsequently transferred to the museum. These had originally been part of the Correr, Molin and Cicogna collections and included some of the finest examples of Renaissance work.
The collections were reordered in 1932 on the basis of more contemporary exhibiting criteria by Giulio Lorenzetti and Nino Barbantini. In the same year, the Ministry of Education's head office for antiquities and fine arts authorised the move of a nucleus of archaeological glass from the Loewy collection and from a tomb in Salizzole (Verona) to the museum on deposit. Works from the museum of San Donato in Zadar were then added in 1963, and together these make up the present archaeological section.
The museum is housed in the old Palazzo dei Vescovi di Torcello, of which it originally occupied only a few rooms. This old patrician residence was built in the typical style of flamboyant gothic, of which traces remain in the column with capital, discovered in the atrium during restorations on the ground floor in 1960, and the windows overlooking the courtyard at the back.
The *palazzo* formerly belonged to the noble Cappello family and was bought by the Giustinian family from Francesco Benzon. When the episcopal see of Torcello was abandoned, the bishop Marco Giustinian turned it into his private residence and had it completely renovated to a plan by the architect Antonio Gaspari, a student of Baldassare Longhena. Gaspari modernised the interior and transformed the old gothic facade into its current baroque form, completing the work in 1707.
The building was subsequently taken over by the Venice patriarchate and then sold to the Murano City Council for use as its chambers in 1805.
The present layout is the result of various works to the exhibition rooms (1979), the ground floor, with the porticoed courtyard and garden (1999) and the facade (in 2005).

The garden with the Santi Maria e Donato basilica in the background and the Canneto *installation (1998) by the sculptor Pino Castagna.*

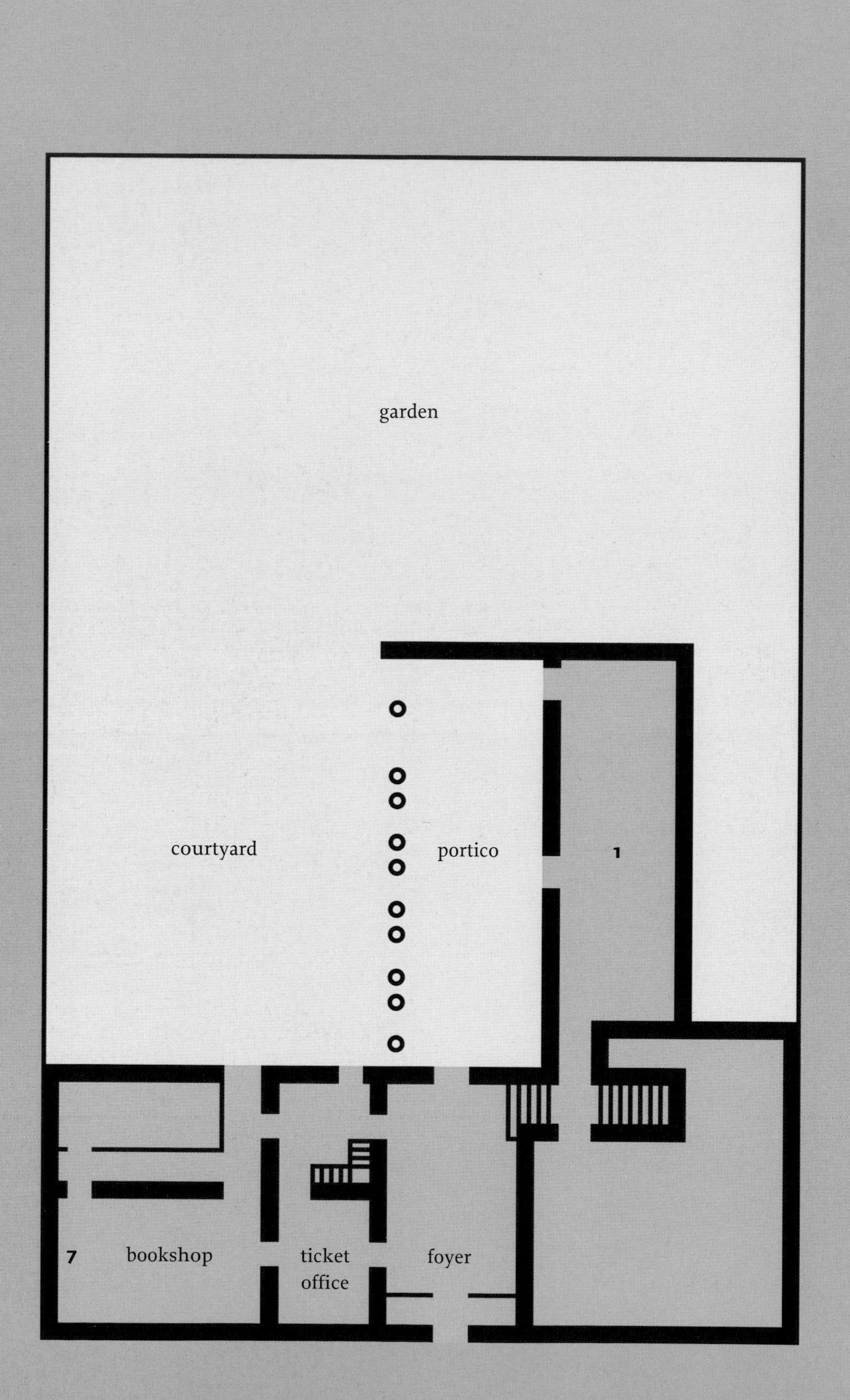
garden
courtyard
portico
1
7
bookshop
ticket
office
foyer

1 The archaeological collection
2 The Middle Ages and the Renaissance
3 The sixteenth century
4 The seventeenth century
5 The eighteenth century
6 The hall:
nineteenth-century glass
and twentieth-century glass
7 Contemporary glass

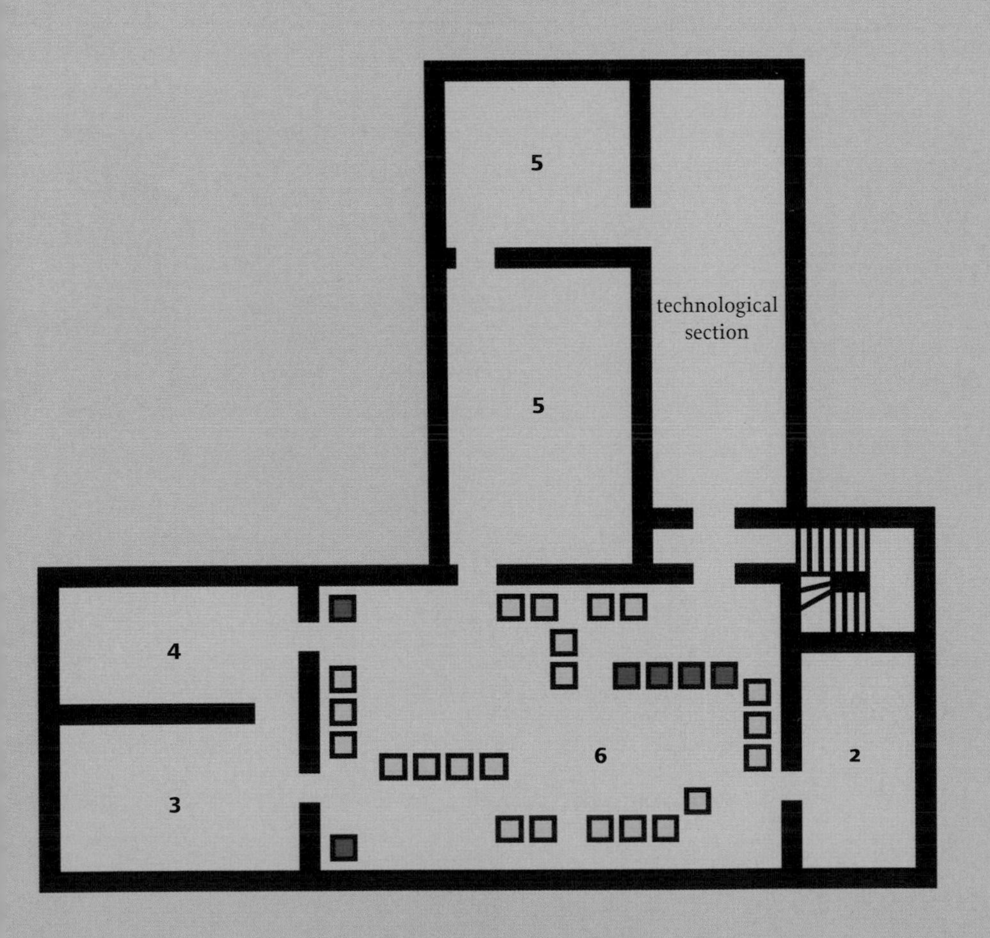

The oldest document in which reference is made to glassmaking in the lagoon area dates from 982. It mentions a certain Domenico *fiolario* as a witness in a donation deed. The term *fiolario* signifies glass-maker, as *fiole* were bottles in blown glass with a long neck and round body.
The nickname *fiolario* also appears in subsequent documents (1083, 1090, 1158), so it may be inferred that glass works were already active in the lagoon area in the tenth and eleventh centuries, though it is not possible to guess exactly what they produced.
Only from the thirteenth century does the number of documents on glass-makers increase, allowing a fairly precise picture of their activity to be drawn.
In 1224 the glass-makers were already united in a trade corporation, also known as an *Arte*, which was endowed with a statute in 1271: the *Capitulare de Fiolariis*, also known as a *Matricula* (register), or *Mariegola* in vernacular, setting out the rules governing the activity of the *Arte*. A new edition of the *Mariegola*, written in the vernacular, appeared in 1441, followed by others through to 1766.
In addition to bringing together those who had acquired the right to practise a certain profession, agreeing to comply with certain demands required by the state, the *Arte* in Venice also had the connotations of a *Scuola*. These were religious or welfare societies, whose representatives were required to take part in important public ceremonies. Indeed, Martino da Canal notes in *La Cronique des Veniciens* that the glass-makers paraded on the occasion of the election of Doge Lorenzo Tiepolo in 1268, richly costumed and preceded by their sign.
The *Arte* was governed by a steward, elected annually by the members of the corporation, and assisted in his work by officials or 'judges' who together managed the craft community.
Additional information on the operations and life of the *Arte* and the tools used by the glass-makers in medieval times is provided by the *Atti dei Podestà di Murano* (Venice, State Archive) from 1291 to 1351.
A decree of the Great Council of 1291 ordered that all furnaces be moved to Murano as a safeguard against fires in Venice city. Most of these were in any case already concentrated there, particularly along what is now known as the Rio dei Vetrai, then the Rio di Santo Stefano; St Stephen was the first patron of the glass-makers and appears in the illuminated first letter of the first page of the *Mariegola* of 1441, to be replaced by St Nicholas only in the late fifteenth century.
At the beginning of the fourteenth century there were at least 12 glass works producing blown glass in Murano. The documents of the time mention carafes for oil and wine (*buçae*), measuring recipi-

ents for public retailing, marked by a thread of blue glass at the spout, *inghistere*, carafes with a long neck and fairly similar to the *fiole*, glasses (at first known as *moioli* or *ciati*, and only later, in 1411, *goti*, a dialect term still in use in Venice and finally, in 1437, glasses), beakers, salt cellars and cups.

The production of flat glass for windows, made up of several discs joined with lead, must have been considerable in the Middle Ages. They are recorded in a decree of the Grand Council of 1368 in which it is forbidden 'to shoot pellets with bows in the city of Venice, or to break glass windows.' The use of glass in the windows was still cause for astonishment many years later (1581) to Francesco Sansovino, who pointed out, as a sign of the city's opulence, that 'all the windows close, not with cloth coverings of waxed canvas, or paper, but with very fine, white glass, enclosed in frames of wood and held with iron and lead, not only in the palaces and apartment blocks, but in all places, no matter how mean.'

The archive documents show that, from the Middle Ages, numerous exports of Murano glass were made to the Eastern Latin Empire (1276), to the current Dubrovnik, Bulgaria and Rhodes. But little material evidence of the production in these first centuries of work has come down to us, and what there is fragmentary. This is because of the eminently utilitarian nature of the glass made, which was liable to breakage as a direct consequence of its daily use, and because of the fragility of the material itself, subject to a process of devitrification due to the lack of a specific stabiliser in the glass mix. Pliny (AD 23-79) recounts in his *Naturalis Historia* how glass was discovered by chance by some Phoenician merchants several millennia before the birth of Christ. Finding themselves on the sandy banks of

1. Murrine *and polychrome striped cups, first century AD.*

[1.]

[2.]

a Syrian river, the merchants had lit a fire using cakes of natron (natural soda consisting mainly of sodium carbonate), which, with the sand and the effect of the heat, gave rise to glass.
Indeed, the two basic materials initially used for glass in Murano were quarried siliceous sand, which was the vitrescent substance, and soda, used as a flux.
The quarried siliceous sand, which now comes mainly from quarries in Fontainebleau, could also be taken from powdered river pebbles. Those from the Ticino river, of a guaranteed purity and capable of producing colourless glass, were used from the mid-fourteenth century. Soda, which could be obtained not only from natron, but also from the sodic ashes of plants from the Mediterranean shores, in old documents is referred to as *lume gatino*. The ash-grey *lume di Sorìa*, from Syria, was rated particularly highly, while the darker one from Alexandria in Egypt was less popular. Soda is now almost exclusively obtained by chemical processes.
Another fundamental raw material for glass is calcium carbonate, or more commonly lime, which acts as stabiliser. It not only has the property of lowering the melting temperature of the vitrescible mixture, but also increases the chemical resistance of the glass and limits its tendency to become opaque. In early times lime was unintentionally introduced to the vitrescible mix, being contained in the ashes of the plants. The vitrescible mix is made up of a vitrescent substance, sand (60-65%); a flux, soda (about 20-25%); and a stabiliser, lime (about 10-15%).

2. Cups blown with the aid of a mould, first century AD.

Broken glass must also be listed among the raw materials. The waste material from processing, once known also as *vitreum*, was collected in a special container to be reused in a new mix. The raw materials today must be dried before reaching a set humidity, then ground, if necessary, to produce the optimum grain size. Once they have been weighed, they are mixed together in a mixer to create a uniform blend, then moved to a single container, known as an *albuol*. The resulting vitrescible mixture is poured into pots, also known as *padelle*, which are circular or oval recipients in a refractory material able to withstand the high temperatures, and placed inside the smelting furnace.

The Murano furnaces and the processes for blowing were originally not very different from those used in ancient Rome. A glass works normally had two or three wood-fuelled furnaces. In the first, also known as the *calchera*, the first casting of the mixture, consisting mainly of flux and vitrescent substance, was made, resulting in a partially vitrified aggregate known as *massa di vetro* (*vitreo de masea*) and then the frit.

The frit, cooled and broken into pieces, was reused in the second furnace along with other raw materials to produce a sufficiently pure vitreous cast. The molten glass was then extracted with big iron spoons, or *cazze*, and poured into a tub of water to cleanse it; the resulting *cotizzo* was then returned to the furnace to become glass ready for working. When the glass piece was finished, it was moved to a third furnace at a lower temperature where it underwent a slow cooling process known as annealing. After the first world war, the wood used to fuel the furnaces was replaced by coal and then fuel oil; since the second world war methane gas has been used.

The annealing furnace was also modified, being converted into a long tunnel lined with bricks and heated independently. The glass to be annealed was placed inside it in iron containers connected to one another and made to move slowly from the hotter end of the furnace to the cooler end. The iron containers have recently been replaced by metal conveyor belts.

Because of the high temperatures of the furnaces, the frit is no longer made. The vitrescible mixture is now poured directly into the pots inside the furnace. Apertures known as *bocche* (mouths) near the pots on the side walls of the furnace allow the vitrescible mixture to be put into the pots and the glass needed for working taken out.

The tools used today to blow glass are not very different from those used in the Middle Ages. The master takes the first amount of glass, or 'posta' from the pot with the blowpipe. The latter has been known by this name only since the nineteenth century, having previously been known as a *ferro*, *ferro forato* or *ferri busi* (hollow tool).

It is a hollow iron pipe, slightly conical at the end used to pick up the glass. This tool is mainly for blowing air into the *posta* (also known as the *bolo* [bole] or *pea*) during the work.
Since the Middle Ages, blowing has been carried out either 'freehand' or with open or closed moulds: the former to give the glass a decorative pattern, the latter to give it a particular shape.
Another very important tool for working blown glass is the *pontello*, mentioned in Murano papers since the early fifteenth century. It is used to support the blown glass being worked when the end previously attached to the blowpipe needs to be worked hot. The *borselle* are pincers of various shapes according to their intended use, for modelling the glass, while the *tagianti* are big scissors for cutting the glass being worked.
Other tools used by the master craftsmen are calipers to check the size; the *paletta* in iron or wood which, often immersed in cold water, serves mainly to smooth the surfaces; and the *supieto*, an iron tool consisting of a small hollow shaft ending in a cone, used to even or reduce the thickness of the blown glass being worked. The *piazza* is the group assigned to working the glass at a furnace and is made up of a master, a *servente* (gunner), a *serventin* (little gunner) and a *garzone* (boy). The master assigns different tasks to his team according to each one's experience and ability. The master usually works at the *scagno* (bench), a seat fitted with two arms, known as *bardelle*, on which to rotate the pipe with the glass attached to make it easier to work.
Before working the blown glass, the right tools must be prepared and the design with dimensions of the piece being made studied.
The work begins with the *levada*, or the removal of a certain quantity of molten glass (*pea* or *bolo*) with the blowpipe. This is lightly blown and marbled on a *bronzin*; that is, it is rolled on a metal plate (once stone) to give it a more or less cylindrical form. The master then begins work with the necessary tools: the *tagianti* and *borselle*, to begin forming the object.
In the course of these operations, seated at the bench, he continues to roll the blowpipe on the *bardelle* (arms) while being helped by the *servente* who, when necessary, blows on the molten glass. Subsequent returns to the furnace allow work to continue on the object until, when it has reached the right dimensions, it is attached to the *pontello* for finishing. This is applied to the opposite side from that of the blowpipe, which is removed with a sharp strike of the *borselle*.
Once the object has been completed, it is placed in the annealing furnace, where it is slowly cooled to guard against permanent stresses that could lead to its breakage. Although the documents allow a fairly clear picture of the work on Murano in the Middle Ages to be drawn, the problem of its origins remains. There may be some foun-

dation in the nineteenth-century theory that the art of blowing glass was brought to the lagoon area by Veneto people from the mainland, particularly from the Roman Aquileia and Altino, who were forced to seek refuge in the islands from the threat of the Barbarians in the fifth century. But the close contacts Venice maintained with the East for many centuries seem to have been quite decisive in its development, particularly on a formal level.
On questions of technique, though, the Murano glass-makers looked mainly to Roman glass. A comprehensive illustration of Roman glass production from the first centuries AD is presented in the archaeological section.

[3.]

3. Small amphorae blown with the aid of a mould, first century AD.

1. The archaeological collection

The room housing the archaeological collection is on the left, at the bottom of the staircase leading to the first *piano nobile*. It contains glass that mainly came from the necropolises of Enona, Asseria and Zadar. These were previously moved to Venice from the Museum of San Donato in Zadar for safekeeping during the second world war, when those territories were part of the Italian state. Italy then agreed to return the cultural assets taken from them to Yugoslavia, following the provisions of the 1947 peace treaty.
After long diplomatic negotiations, however, it was finally agreed that Yugoslavia would give up the archaeological material from the Zadar Museum in exchange for four Roman imperial statues. The glass from the Zadar Museum was placed on deposit at the Glass Museum in 1963.
It contains a vast range of objects: cinerary urns, *balsamari*, bowls, glasses, rings, bracelets, necklaces, bottles, jugs, plates, *gutti*, funnels and *kantharoi* from a fairly wide chronological period between the first century BC and the fourth century AD. Their dating can be no more specific than that of the century, because their tomb context is unknown; the accompanying clay materials and coins in these normally allow more precise dating.
Some cinerary urns in blown glass can be seen in the showcase on the right, near the entrance, with other burial objects intended to contain the ashes of the deceased after their cremation.
The urns, dating from the first and second centuries AD, with some personal grave goods of the deceased, were then placed in cylindrical urns in the area of the necropolis.
The wall showcases contain examples of blown glass from the Roman imperial age made by blowing with and without moulds. The plates, amphora and small cup, from the first century AD, are of particular interest. They were shaped in moulds then faceted by grinding and are based on similar examples in metal.
The mould-blown drop or ashlared goblets and the competition *pocula* (glasses) are typical of imperial glass production and were widespread in many imperial provinces in the first century AD; the latter have good wishes written on them in Greek and were usually made for athletic events.
The *balsamari*, containers for unguents, oils and perfumes, certainly had an important role in the large variety of Roman production. Those with polychrome bands are particularly important, mainly because they were the inspiration for the Murano glass-makers of the nineteenth century, who also tried to imitate the small bowls in millefiori mosaic of the first and second centuries AD.
The *askós*, the drinking horn or rhyton, used to decant liquids, two funnels, a *guttus* used as a dropper, and the wine sampler bent at a right angle at the upper end were probably objects of domestic use.

4. Kantharoi *in blown glass, second half of the first century AD.*

ground floor

Along with the cups, the small urns and plates of different sizes, the square bodied bottles, blown with and without the help of a mould, are interesting as they often have a factory trademark on the base.
The mould was frequently used in the Roman period. This is demonstrated by the numerous jugs or the *balsamari* whose sides may have various kinds of decoration, geometrical, floral or figurative. The so-called *Argonauts'* flask is of particular interest, decorated with episodes from the legend recounted by Apollonius Rodius in the second century. It shows Jason on his ship in search of the golden fleece and the *condottiere* seated beside a tree holding the mythical sheep.
Similar small bottles were blown in double moulds that had the scenes portrayed on their sides in negative to appear in positive on the glass.
The cups with large vertical ribbing are of similar interest from a technical point of view. They were made with the system that was to be known centuries later in Murano as *mezza stampaura*.
The bottle with *barbotine* work, also applied to ceramics, is unique. This method consisted of fusing threads of glass onto the body of

5. Glasses and bottle blown with the aid of a mould, late first century AD.

6. Polychrome cane balsamari *and small* balsamario *in the shape of a date, first century AD.*

[5.]

the object, still attached to the blowpipe, which the master shaped with the pincers.
The forms of the *kantharoi* are derived form the Greek world: cups with base and two handles, at times engraved with a wheel and generally in charming colours. Wheel engraving is also applied to some fragments, possibly parts of cups, with the representations of a goddess, Isis, and hunting scenes. These are portrayed with various depths on a surface previously ground and therefore opaque, along with episodes of circus games, from the first-second centuries AD.
On the right, at the top of the staircase to the first floor is the vaulted room with the technological section. It is dedicated to the processes of preparing and working glass, with the relative tools, as carried out in Murano in the past and today. The section has been set up by the Stazione Sperimentale del Vetro, which is based on the island.

[6.]

Some fragments of medieval glass, dating from between the tenth and fifteenth centuries, are shown in the room with the oldest examples in the museum's collections. They are in the wall showcase in front of the windows and consist of the necks, spouts, bases and sides of bottles, glasses and lamps in a glass with greenish tones caused by impurities in the flux (soda). They were found among the foundations of the nearby basilica of Santi Maria e Donato during excavations carried out in 1975 for its restoration and consolidation. These fragments are of interest because in some cases the original form of the object can be conjectured by comparison with contemporary iconographic sources – mosaics and paintings.

The *inghistera* or bottle, and two glasses in very thin, yellowish glass in the first showcase from the end (7) are of great interest in documenting medieval glass production. They were found during excavations made by the Soprintendenza per i Beni Ambientali e Architettonici di Venezia in the Campo della Chiesa at Malamocco, a hamlet on the Lido and first residence of the doges. The truncated cone glasses and bottle, with long neck and onion-shaped body, decorated with ribbing made by mould blowing, are some of the few finds that are datable, thanks to the ceramic fragments found in the same context; they are from the end of the fourteenth and the beginning of the fifteenth century.

The big truncated cone glass with an aquamarine thread on the brim and the one with big drops on the lower sides, applied hot and drawn with pincers, with two aquamarine threads defining the upper vertical edge, are two of the oldest examples of the island production, in a glass not yet completely purified. The diamonds extending over the whole surface of the former are obtained by blowing in a mould that is still known today as a *baloton*; in the latter, the drop pattern relates to a recurring decoration that was common in the German area during the Middle Ages and Renaissance

[7.]

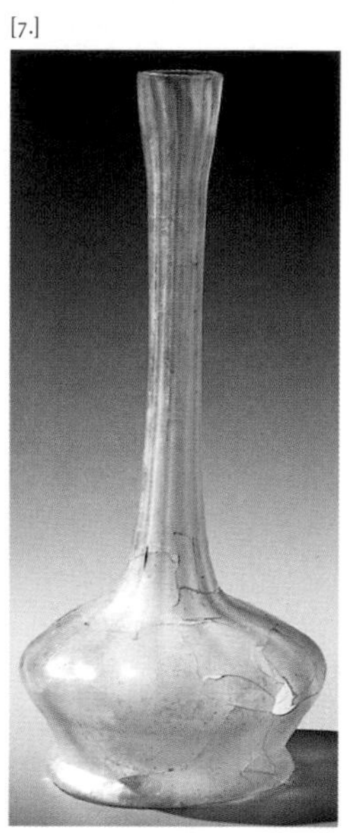

7. Inghistera *with onion shaped body and glasses in yellowish glass, late fourteenth – early fifteenth century. On deposit from the Venice and Lagoon Soprintendenza BAPPSAE.*

8. Jug in crystal decorated with fusible polychrome enamels, with floral shoots, late fifteenth – early sixteenth century.

[7.]

first floor

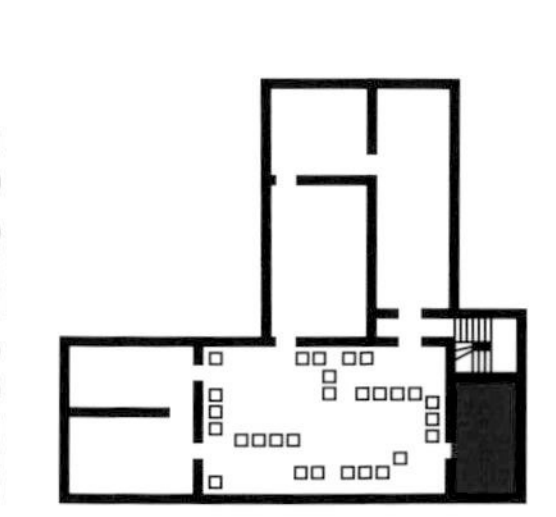

and known as *krautstrunk*. This one was produced in Murano, however, where such models, certainly intended for export, were described as *Teutonics* in early documents. The two objects can be dated to the second half of the fifteenth century. Traces of devitrification caused by insufficient stabiliser in the glass mix are evident in the whitish patina that mars the transparency of the truncated cone glass.

Murano had mainly produced items for everyday use until the middle of the fifteenth century, when a radical change took place. The work began to reach extraordinary levels of artistic expression in items of refined quality and elegance that were to ensure Murano its role of absolute leadership in the manufacture of glass for several centuries.

This renovation was linked to the studies and research carried out by Angelo Barovier (1405-1460), the most celebrated glass-maker of the fifteenth century. Around 1450 he managed to obtain a particularly clear material: by a series of complicated operations, he succeeded in removing the impurities from the sodium ash – the flux in the vitreous mixture – that had marred medieval glass. The result was a pure substance that was also known as 'crystal' and could be colourless or coloured. This discovery made Barovier very famous, such that the Serenissima Repubblica gave him permission to make the new type of glass even during the obligatory closure period of the furnaces, from mid-August to mid-January every year. As a mark of admiration, Francesco Sforza invited him and his son Marino to his court in Milan.

The glass-maker's secrets for making 'crystal' quickly spread, however, and by the end of the fifteenth century this type of glass was being made in all the best studios in Murano. The glass of this period won great acclaim all over Europe, where it adorned the houses

[9.]

[10.]

[11.]

[12.]

and tables of the nobility and rich middle classes. The most significant examples of work from the second half of the fifteenth century are the pieces decorated with fusible polychrome enamels. Such decorations were made at the glass works and required the intervention of specialised painters, whose presence on the island is documented from the end of the thirteenth century. Once shaped and cooled, the piece was entrusted to the painter, who decorated it by brush with enamels consisting of powdered glass mixed with coloured pigments, metal oxides and substances or essences of grease. The object was then returned to the furnace to melt the enamels, which thus became indelible. Only after this stage was the object completed with handles, base and any other accessories, which would have been easily deformed if already attached at the time of the second firing. This decorative technique may be seen in all its variety in numerous pieces in this room. The two single-handled jugs (late fifteenth – early sixteenth century) resting on a short flared foot, have highly coloured plaits of flowers on the body that are repeated on the neck of one of the two examples, while the other is decorated with rows of scales, an originally Oriental motif that often appears in glass of this period (8).
White and gold enamel scales cover the sides of a blue bowl (10) in the next showcase, while a lion and bird are shown between interwoven dolphins inside the typical motif of plaited flowers on the fragmented goblet with flared body and base (11). This piece is important as it was found among the foundations of the bell tower in St Mark's square when it fell in 1902. It was in a layer known to date from around 1500, so allows not only this piece but other similar ones in European and American museums to be dated to that period.
Because of their recognised expertise, the Murano studios received numerous commissions from the most prestigious families and most important people, not only in Italy. This is shown by the coats of arms that are a certain indication of ownership: that of the Barbarigo family, surmounted by the ducal crown, stands in the centre of a plate with ribbing applied by *mezza stampaura* and decorated with vegetal motifs in enamels and gold (12). Marco and his brother Agostino Barbarigo were doges of Venice, one after the other, between 1485 and 1501, so this is the period to which the piece may be dated.

9. Cesendello *decorated with flat tiles in fusible polychrome enamels and gold with the Tiepolo coat of arms topped with the ducal crown, late fifteenth – early sixteenth century.*

10. *Bowl in blue glass decorated with fusible polychrome enamels and gold with scale patterns, late fifteenth century.*

11. *Broken goblet decorated with fusible polychrome enamels with a lion and bird supported by dolphins, late fifteenth century.*

12. *Plate in crystal with heavy ribbing obtained using the* mezza stampaura *technique. The decoration in fusible polychrome enamels has the Barbarigo coat of arms in the middle, surmounted by the ducal crown, late fifteenth century.*

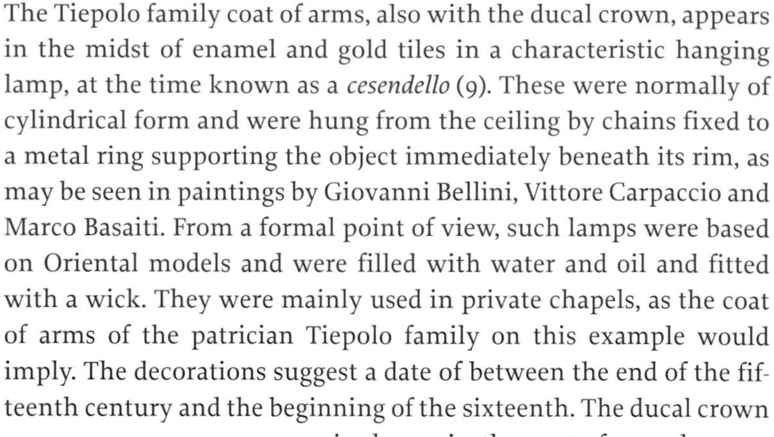

13. Acquereccia *in the shape of a small craft, first half of sixteenth century.*

14. Cup on base, with coat of arms of Sixtus IV della Rovere in fusible polychrome enamels, second half of fifteenth century.

The Tiepolo family coat of arms, also with the ducal crown, appears in the midst of enamel and gold tiles in a characteristic hanging lamp, at the time known as a *cesendello* (9). These were normally of cylindrical form and were hung from the ceiling by chains fixed to a metal ring supporting the object immediately beneath its rim, as may be seen in paintings by Giovanni Bellini, Vittore Carpaccio and Marco Basaiti. From a formal point of view, such lamps were based on Oriental models and were filled with water and oil and fitted with a wick. They were mainly used in private chapels, as the coat of arms of the patrician Tiepolo family on this example would imply. The decorations suggest a date of between the end of the fifteenth century and the beginning of the sixteenth. The ducal crown is shown in the coat of arms because some members of the family had been doges in the thirteenth century. The tile and gold decorations on the sides of the lamp are applied in a particularly elegant manner.

[13.]

Cups on bases in the next showcases are distinguished by other coats of arms: that of the Zaguri family, which received Venetian citizenship in the early sixteenth century, for example, and that of Pope Sixtus IV della Rovere, on the papal throne between 1471 and 1484, with the keys and shield surmounted by the classic triple crown in the centre of a simple decoration with small dots and lines in polychrome enamels (14). The object is part of a rich collection of Venetian glass recently donated to the Glass Museum by Dr Vito Manca.

The popularity of enamel and gold decorations between the end of the fifteenth century and the beginning of the sixteenth is also shown by the rosettes marking the edges of a plate and a big cup on bases (15). The latter also documents another technique used in Murano, the *mezza stampaura*, which has been known since Roman times and is still used today. It consists of placing the lower half of a blown object, still attached to the blowpipe, in a vitreous half mould that has been imprinted in an open mould with negative ribbing. Additional blowing into the object causes the formation of ribbing, in positive, with varying degrees of density and relief.

[14.]

The transparency of uncoloured glass was particularly accentuated in the first years of the sixteenth century, in cups on bases and goblets, both by the application of blue glass threads, a colour obtained with cobalt, and by particular effects obtained using *mezza stampaura* reliefs or a mould known as a *baloton* to create diamond shapes.
A piece that attracted great admiration in its day because of its originality was the *mesciacqua* in the form of a small craft (13). There is probably no truth in the tradition that it was made by Armenia Vivarini, daughter of the painter Alvise, but glass of this type did appear at the Venetian fair of Ascension in 1525, where the Murano glass-makers were permitted to exhibit their most recent production, as noted by Marin Sanudo in his *Diarii*. The blown glass hull is completed with aquamarine threads and lozenges applied hot, and by complex perforations made by hand with consummate skill and precision, alluding to the rigging of the stern sails. Along with blowing, one of the specific qualities of glass made in Murano was, and remains, free-hand work, which requires undoubted skill and expertise to attain such perfect results.
Craft of this type were very successful and widely made, particular-

ly in the glass works of Holland, which made glass *à la façon de Venise* using Italian craftsmen, among whom glass-makers from Murano played an important part.

The *mezza stampaura* technique is particularly shown off by segments in opaque white glass, known as milk glass, arranged along the ribbing of a cup with blue base (16). This kind of decoration was obtained by wrapping white threads around the glass immediately after it had been removed from the mould. Further blowing and the consequent expansion of the glass caused the threads to shatter, and to be deposited in segments along the raised sections. Milk glass was used in the fifteenth century only for mosaics and enamels; it was obtained by adding manganese bioxide, as a decolourant, and lead and tin, as an opacifier, to the crystal frit: the partially vitrified spongy aggregate produced by heating the mix of flux (ash) and vitrescent substance (sand).

[15.]

[16.]

The method of blowing milk glass was discovered in the second half of the fifteenth century, and it seems that Angelo Barovier may have been involved in this. Only a few more than a dozen pieces of blown milk glass are known of from between the end of the fifteenth century and the start of the sixteenth. They are all decorated with religious or mythological scenes in fusible polychrome enamels, or with female and male busts inspired by contemporary paintings or engravings. This type of glass was also used to imitate Chinese porcelain, which had arrived in Europe shortly after the mid-fifteenth century and was considered very precious, such that in documents of the period milk glass is also called *porcellanacontrafacta* (fake porcelain). The known examples, glasses, goblets and cups, are held in various European and American museums.

The cup in the showcase between the two windows is certainly one of the more noteworthy examples of glass making in Murano from the end of the fifteenth century (17). It is in very pure, intense blue glass and decorated with two portraits, one male and one female, within medallions, in fusible polychrome enamels. A procession of young girls toward the fountain of youth, or of love, is shown between these, along with the girls bathing in it. These are typical themes of Renaissance iconography that frequently appear both in paintings and book illustrations.

The role Angelo Barovier played in glass technology was incorrectly interpreted by scholars between the end of the nineteenth century

15. Big cup on base in crystal with ribbing obtained using the mezza stampaura *technique. Rosettes in fusible polychrome enamels run under the edge, early sixteenth century.*

16. Cup on base in blue glass, mould blown, decorated with segments in milk glass along the ribbing, sixteenth century.

17. Coppa Barovier *in blue glass with fusible polychrome enamel and gold, 1470-1480.*

and the beginning of the twentieth. He was thought to have been a decorator and was attributed the ornamentation of the object that, since then, has been known as the *Coppa Barovier.* Furthermore, because of the two portraits and themes of good wishes, it was thought to have been made for a wedding, and hence the name 'nuptial' that long accompanied the work. The cup is a unique example; the images, created with great skill and refinement, suggest a date between 1470 and 1480, making it one of the oldest examples of those decorated with fusible polychrome enamels.

[17.]

It is not possible to trace a precise turning point in the production of Murano glass between the end of the fifteenth century and the start of the sixteenth. The techniques and formal approaches developed continued to be used and in general no great variations occurred.
The most significant production on the island was of crystal and its new related technological applications. Thanks to its purity, crystal was seen as the ideal material for expressing the canons of harmony and essentiality that, in the course of the century, the applied arts, and therefore glass, were inspired to show off alongside their bigger sisters, architecture and painting.
Such criteria seem obvious in the series of goblets in the first showcase in the room. All their parts, from the bowl to the stem and the foot, were blown separately and then joined hot with the frequent insertion of rings or small globes, also known as *gropi*, between the bowl, called the *bevante*, often conical but at times more elaborate, and the stem (18).

[18.]

18. Goblets in crystal with baluster and gropi *stem, sixteenth century.*

19. Reliquary, from the church of San Martino, Burano, decorated with diamond engravings and polychrome enamels applied cold, second half of sixteenth century.

The 'baluster' goblets in which the stem takes the typical shape of the architectural baluster are typical of the sixteenth century (20). Their calibrated proportions control the relations between their constituent parts, which at times may be blown with the aid of a mould, and therefore have light ribbing; the insertion of a stem in a contrasting colour, like blue, was also common. It is precisely these goblets, along with very transparent vases and evanescent jugs, that were portrayed in contemporary paintings by Titian, Paolo Veronese and Tintoretto.
One of the most effective of the new decorative techniques associated with crystal was that of diamond engraving. This had already been known in Roman and medieval times, but was revived in Murano by Vincenzo d'Angelo. His family had been active on the island since the second half of the fourteenth century and had adopted a rooster as the sign of its studio, which thus became known as d'Angelo dal Gallo.
Vincenzo had been decorating the borders of mirrors, produced by his family, with diamond engraving since 1534, and in 1549 he obtained from the Senate the privilege that 'for the next ten years, no one else but he may use the method he rediscovered for engraving glass, without his permission.'
The term 'engraving' refers specifically to diamond engraving,

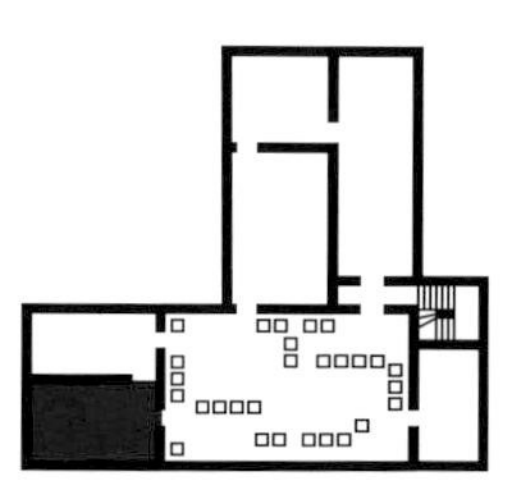

which was widely used in the sixteenth and seventeenth centuries. It involved the tracing of vegetal, geometrical or animal decorations on the basis of a precise drawing, which were the perfect means of highlighting the transparency and purity of the crystal. The result was a subtle play of spaces and solids with effects similar to those of lace, which not by chance was very popular at the time in Venice. It is not possible to certainly attribute any of the examples decorated with this technique to Vincenzo d'Angelo as, once his privilege had expired, it was widely used on the island and remained so in subsequent centuries.

Particularly fine examples of engraving appear on a goblet with lobed cup whose mould blown stem is decorated with lion protomes, while a big tray with base, also known as a fruit stand, is crossed by vegetal and animal motifs drawn with fresh naturalism that suggest a date from the late sixteenth century or the first half of the seventeenth.

20. Goblet in crystal with baluster stem and gropo, and mould blown bowl, late sixteenth, early seventeenth century.

21. Cup and compote decorated respectively with the Holy Lamb and a heraldic eagle along with vegetal motifs, diamond engraved, late sixteenth century.

22. Goblet decorated with diamond engraved vegetal motifs, second half of sixteenth century.

[20.]

[21.]

[22.]

[23.]

23. Small basin, bucket and fruit stand in 'ice glass', late sixteenth century.

24. Large plate decorated with polychrome enamels applied cold on the reverse; the central decoration shows Apollo and the Muses, *the gold bouquets on the edge are interrupted by figurative panels, second half of sixteenth century.*

25. Plate in retortoli *filigree, late sixteenth – early seventeenth century.*

The skill of the Murano engraver is confirmed in two charming examples: a big cup, of quite elegant line and proportions, in which the figure of the Holy Lamb appears between the vegetal patterns along the sides; and a compote with lid that has an eagle in heraldic position between racemes of leaves and flowers. It has small handles decorated with *morise*, which applies to the ornamental vitreous threads worked with special pincers known in glass jargon as *borselle da pissegar* (21).

Objects of every kind were decorated with engraving: small cups, saucers, cruets and small and large goblets (22).

Along with diamond engraving, the same object was at times also decorated with other techniques, as in the case of the reliquary from the church of San Martino di Burano, in which traces of gilding and cold painting are also evident (19).

The shapes of sixteenth-century glass were often applied to other objects in metal or ceramic, such as the jug with elegant, slender handles and sinuous spout, in very pure crystal glass, which often appears reproduced in paintings of the time.

The work of the glass studios was distinguished by many completely new decorative techniques in the sixteenth century, which is for this reason regarded as the golden age for Murano production. So-called cold painting had an important place among these, especially for purely ornamental objects. It was applied on the reverse side of the object and did not require annealing, but this means that the

decorations are prone to fading; indeed, it is extremely rare for these to come down to us intact. This technique was often applied to decorate large objects, such as big plates, cups and basins, with historical, allegorical or mythological subjects. Specialist painters, closer to the sixteenth-century figurative world than that of the glass works, made reference to subjects that were well known both in painting and etching, often reproduced quite faithfully.
An example of this is the big plate of fairly simple form, in which the enigmatic *Dream of Raphael* appears, taken from a 1506-1507 etching by Marcantonio Raimondi, who also inspired other renowned Venetian artists of the century, such as Giulio Campagnola, Giorgione and Titian. The images on another large plate, blown using the 'mezza stampaura' technique, refer rather to the mythological world: *Apollo and the Muses* are shown, with gilt friezes and racemes on the edge alternating with figurative panels (24). *The Carriage of Bacchus* is shown on the bowl of a tall goblet with lion protome stem, and the *Myth of Neptune* depicted on a basin reconstructed from numerous fragments.

[24.]

[25.]

They are all works that can be dated to around the mid-sixteenth century, as can some more simple decorations, such as the vine shoots arranged on the body of an elegant bucket or the geometrical patterns on the bowl of a tall goblet supported by a baluster stem with *gropi*.
Another kind of glass created in the sixteenth century is 'ice glass'. The 1570 inventory made by Bartolo d'Alvise, who owned a glass studio in Murano known as the Tre Mori, includes 'un sechielo a giazo con un fil d'oro.'
The glass, now also known simply as 'ice', has a translucent but not transparent surface crossed by numerous apparently continuous cracks that make it look like ice. This effect is still achieved by the same method, of immersing the still hot, semi-finished glass in cold water. The sudden change of temperature causes cracks to appear on the surface, which are then partially closed by returning the object to the furnace. It is not known exactly when this technique was invented, but it probably dates from mid-century. This kind of glass was very popular in Holland, where Murano craftsmen had moved to work in

local glass works producing *à la façon de Venise*. The fairly sophisticated texture of 'ice' glass makes it ideal for simple, linear forms without decorative elements, apart from edging in blue glass or the hot application of a few decorations in the form of lion protomes. The quality of the material is clearly displayed in the blue-edged bucket and the simple fruit stand, while the small basin with graceful handles worked by pincer already shows a clear tendency toward more elaborate forms that foreshadow the seventeenth century (23).
The most charming and successful technique applied to glass in this century was filigree. It was introduced by Filippo Catani, who came to Murano in 1483 where he opened a glass studio under the sign of a *sirena* (mermaid), from which his whole family was from then on known as Serena.
In 1527 Filippo and his brother Bernardino requested and were granted a ten year privilege from the Serenissima Repubblica to be able to work a new kind of glass of Filippo's creation *a facete con retortoli a fil non mai più fatto*, or in bands with twisted threads never previously made. This was the beginning of a technique still widely used in Murano, where it is commonly known as *filigrana a retortoli* (twisted filigree): the crystal is decorated with parallel bands of threads in milk glass or variously coloured glass, with different weaves. It is a hot decorating technique of applying transparent glass canes containing opaque or coloured white threads that may be straight or variously woven, in which case they take the name of *retorti* or *retortoli* canes. The resulting glass is also known as *zanfirico*, the dialect form of the surname Sanquirico, an antiques dealer who commissioned Murano glass-makers to produce many copies of antique glass with this technique in the nineteenth century.

[26.]

[27.]

Filigree glass was already being marketed in 1540: in that year Domenico Bertolusso de la Nave, who managed a shop in Milan, recorded objects with *retortoli* decoration among other objects arriving from Venice.
A few years later, in 1545, this type of decoration was joined by *reticello* (mesh) glass in the *Mariegola dell'Arte*. It has a dense weave of threads arranged to form a net, with a small bubble of air within each diamond. *Reticello* filigree requires specific, complex procedures involving the use of two cylinders, one closed, the other open, in which the white and coloured threads have been arranged diagonally in opposing directions with the necessary twists. The closed

26. Cup on base in retortoli *filigree, mid-sixteenth century.*

27. Tray on base, with milk glass threads alternating with retortoli *canes, late sixteenth century.*

28. Mould blown fruit stand in retortoli *filigree, late sixteenth – early seventeenth century.*

cylinder is inserted into the open one and blown until they completely adhere to one another. The result is a decoration in the form of a diamond containing a bubble of air, because the threads remain in relief on the surface of the inner glass. In order to obtain blown glass with filigree decoration, the canes, both straight and woven, are arranged on a metal plate and heated in the furnace. They are then collected in a glass bole attached to the blowpipe so as to create an open cylinder, which the craftsman then proceeds to close with scissors known as *tagiante tonda.* When a diagonal arrangement of the decorative pattern is required, he must rotate the blowpipe resting on the bar with one hand, while with the other he holds the part of the closed cylinder with the scissors and keeps it in traction. He then proceeds with the normal blowing operations and forming of the desired object.

The glass produced by the Serena studio is frequently mentioned in archive documents from the second half of the sixteenth century. But Filippo's skill was already well known: in 1521 the Marquise of Mantua asked her ambassador in Venice to send her glass 'with the mark of the mermaid'. In 1525, Marin Sanudo then mentioned Catani, along with Anzolcto Barovier and Francesco Ballarin, in his *Diarii* as makers of 'very beautiful work' presented at the Ascension fair of that year. The Serena studio was in full operation until the mid-seventeenth century; from 1687, *retortoli* and *reticello* glass were more generically known as filigree.

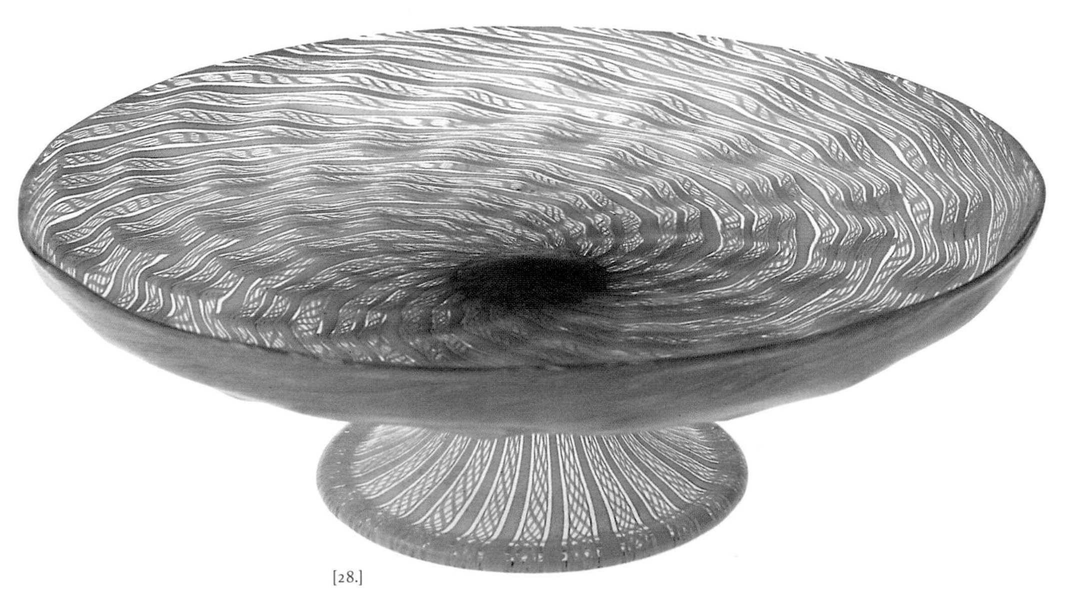

[28.]

Some excellent examples of this technique are displayed in the wall showcases. The *retortoli* variant was expertly applied in a big goblet, dating from the mid-sixteenth century, of singular linear form and balanced proportions, in which a baluster stem with milk glass bands supports a bowl with milk glass, amethyst and crystal canes woven in concentric circles; in a plate with three different weaves of filigree arranged radially – probably from a slightly later date toward the end of the sixteenth century (25); in the goblet, the cup (26) and the fruit stand, or tray with base, which shows how the difficult filigree work could also be associated with mould blowing, evident in the swelling on the vitreous material (28); and, finally, in the tray with base, with alternate threads of milk glass and *retortoli* canes, dating from the mid-sixteenth century and donated to the museum by Vito Manca (27).

29. Large plate in reticello *filigree, late sixteenth century.*

30. Bucket and compote in reticello *filigree, late sixteenth century.*

31. Phial, vase, jugs and goblets decorated with festoons *or* feathers *in milk glass, late sixteenth – early seventeenth century.*

The objects in *reticello* work are also distinguished by their outstanding quality. This very difficult technique required special expertise, as demonstrated in the quite large plate (29), the big compote with lid surmounted by a pinnacle handle, the bucket and the carafe, whose edge has been shaped hot with the expert use of pincers, dating from the end of the sixteenth century or the early years of the seventeenth (30).

[29.]

Despite this great variety of new glass materials, the sixteenth-century masters certainly did not abandon crystal, applying techniques to show off its purity, such as mould blowing and gilding, often restricted to the stem enhanced with masks applied hot, or the use of a glass rod in a contrasting colour, often blue; this combination was to have an important role in the following century. Towards the end of the century, but especially in the next one, a new method of applying the white rod of milk glass became popular. It was wrapped around the sides of the blown object, then combed with a special tool known as a *manareta* to create a festoon pattern. This glass was used to create a great number of forms: bowls, goblets, bottles, cruets and medicine bottles with stopper, all normally finished with a cane of blue glass (31).

[30.]

[31.]

The new types of glass produced in the sixteenth century were also widely used in the following one, which presents problems from a stylistic point of view that have not yet been completely resolved. The glass-makers of Murano generally seemed to stay with sixteenth-century forms, so it is extremely difficult to give a precise dating for a good number of examples, with a possible vacillation from the end of the sixteenth century to the beginning of the eighteenth.

The recipe book belonging to the family of the Darduin glass-makers is extremely useful for information on glass compositions, with recipes from both the sixteenth and seventeenth centuries. Valuable indications on the artistic aspect are provided by some designs in the volumes of Giovanni Maggi's *Bichierografia*, where the Roman painter reproduced not only forms of his own invention, but also the glass in the collection of Cardinal del Monte, datable to between the end of the sixteenth century and the beginning of the seventeenth. These are then supplemented by the drawings of an anonymous designer in the *Libro del Serenissimo Signor Principe Luigi d'Este*, a general of the Serenissima Repubblica in 1617.

These iconographic sources demonstrate the obvious liking of this century's glass-makers for bizarre forms that were almost never functional and therefore entirely decorative. The pieces also contain numerous ornamental elements that, once again, highlight the virtuosity of the master glass-makers.

Several small animals in blown glass – sea horses (32), a dragon, a mouse – are notable for their extravagance, but they are not solely decorative: their function as oil lamps is indicated by the presence of one or two spouts for oil and the wick.

The series of cruets (33), with or without spout, with an abundance of masks and lozenges, often in contrasting colours, is almost exclusively ornamental; as are the small cubic bottles (34), or occasional-

32. Oil lamp in the shape of a small horse with two spouts, one on the tail and one in the body, seventeenth century.

33. Small cruet with crested handle, decorated with pastilles and masks applied hot, seventeenth century.

first floor

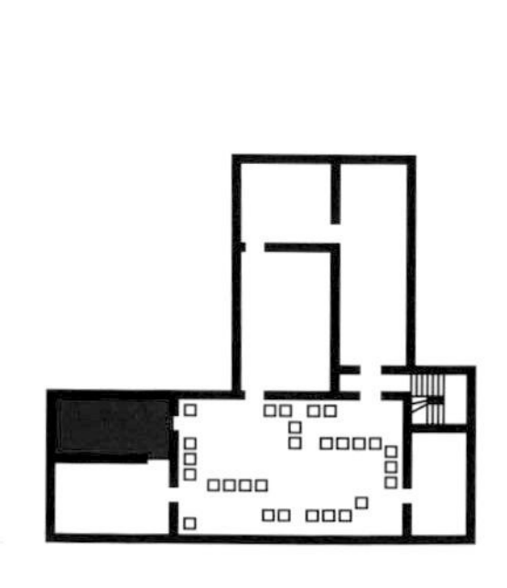

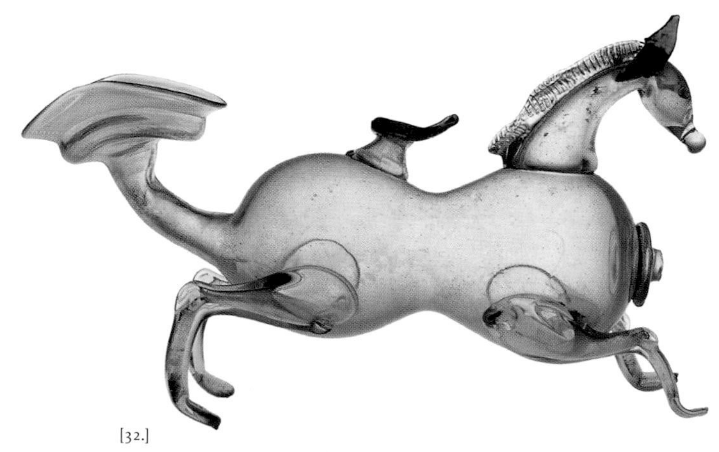

[32.]

[34.]

[35.]

34. Small shell cruets, flower goblet and small bottles in cubic form and with lobed body, seventeenth century.

35. Crystal goblets in unusual shapes, seventeenth century

ly hexagonal ones, whose edges are marked by threads applied and worked with pincers to give them a wavy motion, the *morise.*
The goblets are typical of this century, in a form not unlike those of the previous century, but marked by 'fins' applied to the stem, consisting of a glass thread wrapped around in spiral fashion and overlapped by another, usually in contrasting colours and worked with pincers.
The creativity and imagination of the glass-makers is usually most fully expressed in the structure of the goblet: unusual forms distinguish both the stems, in spirals or declining globes, and the asymmetrical cups. The latter often consist of choked bulbs that suddenly open into a corolla, decorated at times with small chains, or are narrow and quite elongated. It is difficult to imagine that glass of this kind could have had any other function than to astonish and show off the virtuosity and technical skills of the masters (35).
Diamond engraving continued to be widely used in various kinds of production, but tended to take on a more naturalistic style with elegant floral racemes, which, given the evident liking for colour, were often crowned by a chain in aquamarine glass applied hot.
The forms of the small jars with long necks and two or more channels merging into one, or with bodies marked by constrictions, similar to the German *kuttrolf* type, were quite new. They were probably intended to hold precious liquids to be poured out sparingly, drop by drop (36).
A considerable variety of forms was produced in the seventeenth-century, for which moulds were often used, as in the bottle with lobed body and light transverse ribbing, the shell-shaped oil lamps or the vaguely zoomorphic body with flame guard disc (37).
An abundance of decoration is essentially the distinguishing mark of the century, mainly to show off the purity of the glass; the simple, linear forms of the sixteenth century seemed to have been forgotten. In this context a fairly typical object of the period is the goblet with stem in the form of a flower stalk with lanceolate leaves that rise from the base to culminate in a rich flower at the bowl.
Flower goblets were very popular in the Netherlands, made in studios that worked *à la façon de Venise,* but were also produced in Murano, mainly for export.
Blue glass was often used in the seventeenth century, and not only in a complementary way: an example is the mould-blown cruet with shell body, which is a pair with the one in clear glass with thin threads of milk glass, the goblet with blue globe on the stem, and the other with light blue cup, which contrasts pleasantly with the transparent stem decorated with slender fins.
A new kind of vitreous paste, aventurine, also made its appearance. It is a red-brown vitreous paste that in a mass appears as numerous

36. Small vases with squeezing on the neck in kuttrolf *style, seventeenth century.*

37. Lamps in the form of a dragon, seventeenth century.

38. Bottle and cup in chalcedony glass with marks of aventurine, late seventeenth century.

lamellar crystals of copper, similar to stars, from which it is also known as *stellaria*. It is not known who invented it, but it certainly made its appearance in Murano in the first quarter of the seventeenth century, given that in 1626 it is mentioned among the assets of a jeweller who had recently passed on to a better life: 'earrings in aventurine paste, *para* (pair) No. 22; buttons in aventurine paste, various, No. 180; aventurine paste in pieces, *lire* (pounds) 30.'
The composition for this particular vitreous paste was registered for the first time in the recipe book of the glass-maker Giovanni Darduin, compiled between 1644 and 1653. Along with the glass recipes of his father Nicola, it includes others taken from various manuscripts, among which is that of aventurine. He notes that 'it is called aventurine, with good reason, because it arose more by chance than by science', thus pointing out the difficulties of producing this kind of glass, which still distinguish it today.
The technique for making aventurine consists of directly adding to the molten glass small, repeated doses of lead and/or tin, red copper

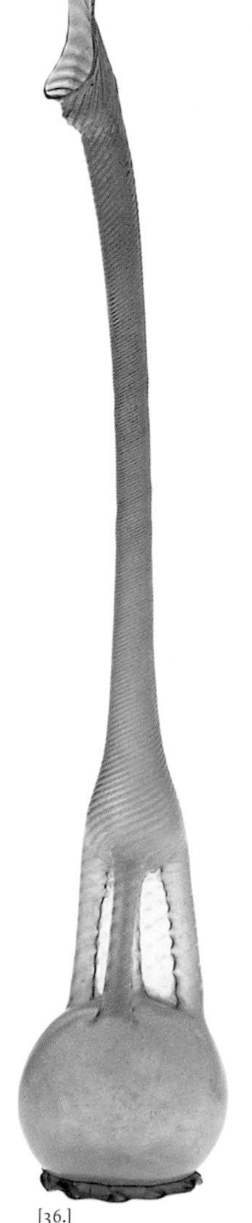

[36.]

[37.]

[38.]

oxide, iron oxide and reducing substances, such as iron flakes. These are to reduce the copper oxide to metallic copper, which precipitates in the glass in crystalline form. At a certain point, the furnace is put out and left closed to cool for one day. When cold, the pot is broken, leaving blocks of aventurine ready for use.

The particular difficulty of making aventurine is pointed out in Darduin's recipe book. He defines it as 'extravagant' and 'delusive', and laments the fact that often, despite several pots being prepared, the outcome is often completely negative because the vitreous paste does not have the necessary uniformity. Because of these problems, it was of course very expensive.

In the seventeenth century aventurine was treated as an ornamental stone, to be squared, turned, faceted, engraved and polished to make buttons, earrings, pill-boxes, brooches, rings and small boxes. The recipe for aventurine was lost between the end of the seventeenth century and the first years of the following one, possibly because of the uncertainty of its production. The vitreous paste was brought to light again by Vincenzo Miotti, a descendant of a glassmaking family working on Murano since the sixteenth century. His father, Daniele, had married one of Giovanni Darduin's daughters and, on the death of Darduin's only son, inherited the recipe and passed it on to Vincenzo. In an account made to the Venetian State Inquisitors in 1721, the latter pointed out that he had 'brought back to life two previously dead Arts in this Noble Dominion, that of making aventurine, a material currently much appreciated in Europe, and that of moulding the mosaics that may save the sumptuous basilica of the venerable St Mark from the ravages of time.'

The secret of making aventurine passed from father to son in the Miotti family until the death of Stefano in 1811, when it was no longer fashionable, resulting in its recipe being once again lost. It was rediscovered in 1820 by the Dal Mistro-Moravia and Pietro Bigaglia companies, but it was another glass-maker of the nineteenth century, Domenico Bussolin, who managed to draw aventurine into canes so it could also be used in blown filigree glass. Until this time it had not been known how this vitreous paste had in the past been blown to be worked as semi-precious stones.

Pietro Bigaglia, who was one of the biggest producers of aventurine in Murano, made the first experiments to make blown glass solely with this material, but it was Antonio Salviati's studio that perfected the technique. In 1869 the most varied forms of blown glass in aventurine made in that glass furnace were presented at the Second Murano Glass Exhibition, known by various names: *avventurinati*, 'with drawn aventurine' or 'with recast aventurine'.

In the seventeenth century, broken into chips and added to the hot glass, then blown and mixed with chalcedony, it gave rise to the

attractive decorative marks that appear in the mould blown bottle with lobed body and the cup with ribbed sides (38).
The charming little cups and graceful sugar bowl with lid, in which the milk glass seems stained or sprayed with polychrome mixes, are from the end of the century (39).
Finally, the bowls with a blue glass bubble inside are typically seventeenth century in shape: the example decorated with festoons complete with lid is particularly elegant (40).
Despite the intense activity of the studios, the seventeenth century was a difficult one for the island, with the onset of problems that were to more heavily influence the production of the following century. Not only had the plague of 1630 taken numerous glass-makers victim, causing serious organisational problems at the studios, but they also had to face considerable difficulties in the supply of raw materials. Furthermore, the economic crisis arising from this provoked a serious fall in the market for Murano glass, such that many glass-makers were reduced to idleness and forced to emigrate. They set up studios working *à la façon de Venise* in other European countries and, in the course of a few years, provided stiff competition for Murano.
Then, in the last quarter of the century, glass-making emerged in other countries that was as refined as that of Murano, but with its own styles and techniques.
In Bohemia, a brilliant, pure potassium crystal, highly suited to engraving, had been developed around the 1670s and quickly won market acclaim. In England, George Ravenscroft had patented lead glass, which was fairly similar to rock crystal and distinguished by its high level of refraction. Spain, which already had a solid glass-making tradition, attracted a large number of the masters emigrating from the island. The Murano craftsmen who went there taught

Pietro Bigaglia, unworked block of aventurine, c. 1845.

the local workforce and, although working in the Venetian tradition, had to adapt to locally preferred shapes and styles, inclined towards an abundance of ornamentation.
Some typical examples of Spanish production from the seventeenth century are shown in the wall display case. The vases known as *jarritos* are typical of Andalusian work. They are always in fairly thick, green glass, with pyriform body decorated with threads, chains, moveable rings and pastilles, and an inverted cone neck onto which four, pronounced, crested handles are grafted. The small flasks with compressed body equipped with stopper are also typical of Andalusia. They were made specifically to be carried in the pocket and decorated with threads defining the sides and with pincer worked shells on the body.
The Murano filigree technique was very popular in Catalonia and often applied to the *cantir*, a recipient with an oval or spherical body and two spouts: one short and wide used to fill the container, and the other long and narrow for drinking. It normally has a big ring

39. Sugar bowl in milk glass with polychrome marks, seventeenth century.

40. Bowl with lid decorated in milk glass festoons, with blue bubble inside, seventeenth century.

[39.]

handle, often surmounted by floral or animal decorations, and stands on a fairly high foot. Multi-spout jars were also widespread in Catalonia. They were variants of the ceramic ones known as *almorratxa*, used to sprinkle rose water at ceremonial occasions.
The decorations, mainly applied, were always an important part of Spanish glass of the time, which is therefore easily recognisable. But for some types, such as the perforated basket, it is very difficult to precisely determine the country of origin.
The keg on a pedestal resting on a tray, probably by a German studio, with deep cuts obtained by grinding, clearly demonstrates the differences both in material and taste between Murano glass and Bohemian crystal.

[40.]

5. The eighteenth century

There was no sign that the problems plaguing the studios in the seventeenth century were to be resolved in the following one. Bohemian and, to a lesser extent, English crystal continued to conquer the markets on which Murano had previously had a kind of monopoly. Even in Venice itself and its territories there was a clear preference for Bohemian products. The result was a major economic crisis that forced many workshops to close over the course of the century.

The glass of the eighteenth century is, however, excellent testimony to the glass-makers' skill, imagination and creativity, in perfect harmony with the preference for colour, splendour and opulence of the period. Not only did it concentrate the whole heritage of forms and techniques developed over the previous centuries, but it also shows the signs of new research carried out to in some way check the foreign competition.

The most prestigious testimony of the first years of this century is offered by the glass collection that Frederic IV of Denmark took back with him to Copenhagen after his stay in Venice in 1709, where it is on display in the Rosenborg castle.

Milk glass had a leading role. It had already been in use between the end of the fifteenth century and the start of the sixteenth, but had since varied in composition, with lead and tin being replaced by lead arsenic to make it opaque. The resulting material was more or less the same as what had previously been made, and lent itself, as in the past, to making imitations of the porcelain from the far-off Orient. This had been made in Europe only from the start of the eighteenth century, and it was no mere chance that Venice showed a clear preference for 'chinoiserie' in that same century.

Milk glass was also at the centre of a new chapter in the history of the glass works. Because of the signature on some of the pieces, their origins can be traced and thus emerge from the anonymity that had always been a hallmark of Murano production. There were two leading studios specialising in this kind of glass: those of the Miotti and the Bertolini families.

The latter, who also had a majolica factory in Murano, were

41. Miotti glass works, plates in milk glass decorated with fusible polychrome enamels showing Joseph and the wife of Potiphar *and* Cain killing Abel, *with the trademark 'Al Gesù Murano 1731' on the rear.*

42. Jug broken during firing and thus factory waste, decorated with a landscape in fusible polychrome enamels and carrying the Miotto glass works trademark, 1736.

first floor

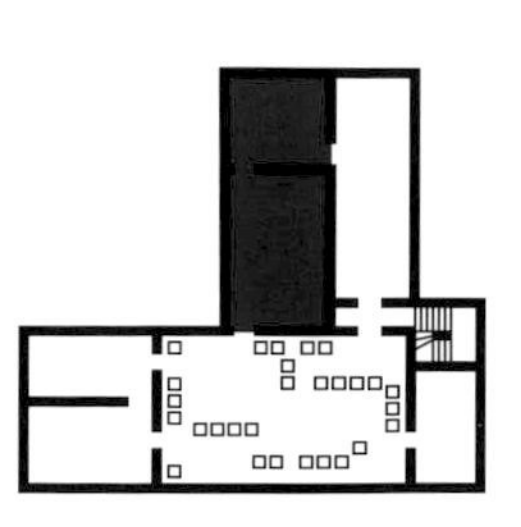

[41.]

[42.]

inscribed in the 'Golden Book' of Murano citizens in 1725. They obtained a 20 year right to produce milk glass decorated with gold, both clear and opaque, which were considered 'distinguished in their manufacture and the charming quality of their decorations'. The bottle, jar and glass with chinoiserie flowers and geometrical patterns are part of this type, though no particular sign allows them to be attributed to Bertolini. This difficulty became even more pronounced when, once their concession had expired, any glass works on the island could make glass of this type. Milk glass was decorated not only with gold and fusible polychrome enamels, but also in monochrome, with scenes often inspired by contemporary engravings, such as on the tobacco case with metal mounting showing episodes from the *Aeneid*.
The milk glass by the Miotti, a family of glass-makers who had been in Murano since the sixteenth century, are often marked with the factory trademark, the monogram of Christ, IHS, which also appears in the sign of the studio, known as 'Al Gesù', and is at times accompanied by the date. Vincenzo Miotti (1644-1729) added the family coat of arms to the monogram: a monkey with an apple, and his ini-

[43.]

[44.]

43. Osvaldo Brussa workshop, glasses decorated with fusible polychrome enamels, second half of eighteenth century.

44. Vase in m ilk glass decorated in blue and gold enamel with Chinese inspired patterns, mid-eighteenth century.

45. Detail of the centre of the big table centrepiece in the form of an Italian garden in crystal and milk glass, c. 1760.

tials, V.M. He was succeeded by his son Daniele (1678-1763), who continued the family tradition of producing enamels, coloured vitreous pastes and milk glass.

Both in the blown milk glass and those in plate form, the decoration with fusible polychrome enamels was carried out by specialist painters who worked for the Miottis, the proprietors being mainly composition technicians and glass-makers.

The flask with the lively floral pattern on the body and elegant geometrical decorations on the neck is from their studio, given that the writing 'Al Gesù di Murano' appears on the base. The small, elegant amphora featuring a monkey holding an apple, perched on a luxuriant stem of leaves, as on the family crest, probably has the same origin.

The same workshop also produced the two rectangular plates with biblical scenes showing *Cain killing Abel* and *Joseph and the wife of Potiphar* within brightly coloured floral frames, marked on the back 'Al Gesù Murano 1731' (41); the jug, whose gaps mark it as factory waste, with a charming painted landscape inspired by those of Marco Ricci and marked 'Al Gesù Murano 1736' (42); the small cup with

[45.]

[46.]

46. Mirror with frame made up of shaped and wheel engraved vitreous plates applied to a wooden structure, eighteenth century.

47. Mirror in gilt wooden frame with a wheel engraved image of Apollo, eighteenth century.

saucer decorated in red ochre with elegant figurines in a landscape, both carrying the monogram IHS.

Milk glass was very popular in the eighteenth century: works of high quality both in terms of manufacture and decoration are held in the most important collections. Even if anonymous, the two vases with orientally inspired decorations in blue enamels are very elegant, as are those with mythological scenes depicted in red ochre (44).

Milk glass was used to make vases, cups, sugar bowls and various other objects, but not always decorated with brightly coloured enamels. At times it was also presented completely free of decoration, simply blown, resulting in small, graceful containers with curled handles.

Fusible polychrome enamel decorations, used both on very simple pieces, generally bottles and glasses of very linear form, were also very popular, ranging from flowers to genre scenes, biblical stories, coats of arms, animals and, above all, birds (43).

Osvaldo Brussa's studio, where his son Angelo also worked, was famous for this work and continued producing through to the early nineteenth century. Osvaldo Brussa himself appears in an eighteenth-century painting in the act of decorating a glass with flowers and birds.

A bottle in milk glass and two glasses offer significant testimony of the spread of this practice to Spain, too. One of them carries the Spanish coat of arms with the lion of Castile and the quartered towers on one side, and the words 'Viva el Reij de España' on the other (second half of the eighteenth century).

The declared preference for colour in this century cannot obscure the interest in vitreous pastes, such as aventurine and chalcedony.

The first was re-presented by Vincenzo Miotti around 1720, who rediscovered the seventeenth-century recipe that had been lost at the turn of the seventeenth century. It had been used in a similar way to semi-precious stones and as such appears in an oval pill box with metal setting. It was also used with chalcedony in glasses and cups of a particular shape, known as *trembleuses*, that fitted into a special recess in their saucer.

[47.]

The veined mixes of various colours used particularly for small quadrangular flasks with metal stopper, at times in the shape of a bird, were very fashionable; filigree was also popular, usually polychrome, giving rise to elegant glass with very imaginative weaves, usually enriched with brightly coloured flowers and filaments applied hot.

The most serious problem faced by Murano in these centuries was, however, the stiff competition of foreign glass, especially that of Bohemia. This was in great demand even in Venice itself. The repeated edicts of the Serenissima against the import and sale of such work had little effect. A temporary solution was found by Giovanni Sola, who managed to import 'crystal paste' from Bohemia in the form of discs, plates, rods and spheres that could be recast, improving the quality of Murano glass and making it more similar to that of Bohemia.

Sola was granted the sole rights for 20 years to import the new lime and potassium based material, which certainly benefited the industry but did not put an end to the arrival of foreign goods in the territories of the Republic, mainly as contraband.

A few years after the expiry of Sola's rights, the solution to the problem was offered by Giuseppe Briati (1686-1772), who made a brilliant, pure potassium crystal that partly checked the Bohemian competition, at least in Venice. In 1736 he asked for a ten year exclusive right to make a 'very fine crystal', specifying that all his efforts, since his youth, had been directed toward the study 'of every kind of crystal with the method of distant countries skilled in such artistry.' He further specified that: 'I arranged to learn this industry by bringing to my home and maintaining for many years the most renowned foreign operators at my own great expenditure of several thousand ducats.'

It is not known whether the glass-maker ever went to Bohemia, but the collaboration of workers from that country and the studies carried out had allowed him to produce a crystal of similar brilliance to the Bohemian. However, unlike the original, it was worked hot in Murano tradition, but could also be engraved by wheel.

The crystal made in Murano was, however, more a free interpretation of foreign crystal than an imitation. It was mainly used to make everyday objects: boxes, salt cellars, small vases, candlesticks, stoups and glass for the table in general, in which the decorations obtained by mould blowing were overlaid with applications of vibrantly coloured bands and polychrome flowers modelled with pincers.

There are only two pieces that are known to have been made by Briati: two cruciform reliquaries decorated with flowers in polychrome vitreous paste, which he donated to the Capuccini monks of the Venetian church of the Redentore, as noted in manuscript sources, and which are still there today. The glass-maker is remembered for a vast

[48.]

[48.]

amount of work. He was renowned for his big table pieces, also known as *deseri* (from the French *dessert*), which the Serenissima Repubblica commissioned from him to decorate the table of the doge on the occasion of banquets held on the public holidays. None of these works have come down to us, but an idea of their function and complexity of construction is evident not only in the small triumph, in the form of a garden with central fountain, in crystal and milk glass, which is actually a nineteenth-century copy of an eighteenth-century original, but especially in the big composition in the centre of the room representing an Italian garden, in crystal and milk glass, made up of numerous pieces (45).
It was purchased for the Glass Museum in the early twentieth century at the public sale of furnishings of the *palazzo* that had belonged to the Morosinis, one of the most important noble families of the Serenissima, and may be dated to circa 1760, given its similarity to the one mentioned in that same year in a page of the *Gazzetta Veneta* by Gasparo Gozzi.
The innovative figures in the Venetian mirrors of the period are also linked to the Briati name. The mirrors were one of the eighteenth-century master glass-makers' most successful products. Large numbers of them were exported and they were highly valued for their artistic quality, despite the competition of French industry. They

48. Phial, goblets and small fruit stand in 'sunflower' glass, early eighteenth century.

[49.]

had been produced there from the end of the seventeenth century, thanks to the Italian glass-maker Bernardo Perotto, by the casting method, which allowed sheets of considerable size.

In Murano mirrors were made by cutting a cylinder of blown glass lengthwise and spreading it out to form a surface, which was then smoothed and polished. The surface was subsequently silvered with a tin amalgam and decorated in the specialist workshops of Venice. It was for the frame above all, rather than the decoration often engraved on the surface, that Venetian mirrors took on a decorative role in home furnishings, such that their function as mirrors seemed to often become quite secondary. Frames made up of polychrome vitreous elements were very popular. The sections were shaped and often very carefully worked, then decorated with ground or engraved enamels and applied to a wooden structure (46). Wooden frames, often gilt or painted, continued to be used, as did those in ceramic, for mirrors whose central section was decorated with a great variety of patterns: from chinoiserie to love scenes, from mythological stories to religious ones and from geometrical decorations to floral ones (47).

49. Plate with wheel engraved Dominican coat of arms, eighteenth century.

50. Glasses with wheel engraved Venetian coats of arms, eighteenth century.

Such characteristics are evident in the mirrors shown in this room and the next one, where the large model is surmounted by a rich pediment of volutes.

A variety of glass that was very successful in the eighteenth century, because of the appeal of its shadings, was opaline, also known as 'sunflower', because it resembled the opal of that name. Examples of its application are the small goblets, the fruit stand with light ribbing and the dainty medicine bottle with lid and handles with *morise* decoration, replicating Renaissance forms previously made in metal (48).

The dark glass that was popular in England was also made toward the end of the eighteenth century, by Giovanni Barbaria, with the aim of averting its import from that country, given the Republic's economic crisis. Bottles intended for keeping wine were the main imports of this glass, but the Murano workshops applied it with their usual imagination to a vast range of objects: cruets, compotes, lamps and miniature amphorae. But such glass was not very popular and thus short lived.

The crystal developed by Briati was particularly suited to being decorated in the style of Bohemian glass, with wheel engravings that at the time were much in demand. Venetian engraved glass can often be mistaken for that of Bohemia, though it can usually be distinguished by shallower carving and a different style of decorative pattern.

The expiry of the rights granted to Briati in 1736 marked the end of his monopoly on Bohemian-style crystal. In any case, several Bohemian engravers had stayed in Venice over the years and had taught the art of grinding, a practice that had achieved good results.

[50.]

[50.]

[51.]

51. Carved and gilt wooden armchair with applications of blue glass plate, mid-eighteenth century.

The plate dating from the mid-eighteenth century, with the crest of the Dominican order surrounded on the edge by rich vegetal patterns and scrolls (49) is probably from the workshop of Vincenzo della Vedoa, where Bohemian engravers were employed; the Mocenigo crest surmounted by the horned ducal headdress in the centre of a corona with vegetable patterns on a large glass is also certainly of Venetian manufacture.
Other glasses of very simple shape, with only slightly rounded sides, are decorated in the same fashion, with a red or blue thread applied to the edge. Portraits of doges with their coats of arms are engraved on the sides while an *osella* is enclosed in the base. This was a coin that the ruling doge had minted each year and given to the nobles (50). It replaced the traditional annual gift of wild ducks hunted in the lagoons under the doge's jurisdiction and known as *osèle*, hence the name of the coin.
Glasses, bottles and plates in Bohemian style glass can be seen on the table, where pharmacy jars are also displayed, along with ornaments and table lamps, or *fiorentine*.
Briati had also begun the practice of decorating furniture with glass. Sources recall his wardrobes, chairs and 'a bureau, or French wardrobe, made entirely of glass.'
This fashion was very widespread, as shown by the fine armchair in inlaid and gilt wood from the mid-eighteenth century, decorated with shaped blue glass plaques (51).
But the glass-maker was most renowned for his chandeliers, known as *chiocche* or *ciocche*, with metal arms covered with tubular, blown crystal elements and decorated with flowers in polychrome vitreous pastes on which the candlesticks stood. They were the Venetian version of the Bohemian chandelier with faceted prisms and took various forms: 'Chinese', when the arms formed a silhouette that vaguely suggested a pagoda; or 'column', when they branched off from small, spiral vertical columns. The ceiling chandelier in the furnished room, though nineteenth-century, is indicative of the forms these could take. They were very successful and became one of the most admired products of the Murano workshops.
Despite the intense activity, the problems and crises that had affected Murano production since the seventeenth century were not resolved by a radical review of the regulations governing it. The fall of the Serenissima Repubblica in 1797, followed by foreign rule and the dissolution of the craft corporations, or *Arti*, in 1806, resulted in most of the workshops on the island closing.

6. The hall: nineteenth- and twentieth-century glass

The glass of the nineteenth and twentieth centuries is displayed in the hall, or *portego*, on the first *piano nobile*, with its numerous windows overlooking the Fondamenta Giustinian and Murano's Grand Canal. The other rooms open onto this one, in keeping with the traditional layout of the Venetian *palazzo*. The ceiling is decorated with a big fresco showing the allegorical *Triumph of St Laurence Giustinian* (1381-1455), the first patriarch of Venice and illustrious forebear of the family that renovated the building between the end of the seventeenth and the early eighteenth centuries. The fresco is by the painter Francesco Zugno (1709-1787), assisted by the *trompe l'oeil* painter Francesco Zanchi (1734-1772) on the architectural sections complementing the main composition. The frieze with the coats of arms of Murano families, however, is modern. The central chandelier of the three big nineteenth-century examples on the ceiling is particularly noteworthy. It is four metres tall, has 60 arms, a maximum diameter of 6.78 metres and consists of 356 pieces.

It weighs 330 kilograms and was made in 1864 by the master glassmakers Giovanni Fuga and Lorenzo Santi. It was presented at the First Murano Glass Exhibition in 1864 and won the gold medal. Some years later it also appeared at the Universal Exhibition in Paris.

52. Pietro Bigaglia, bottle in polychrome filigree, c. 1846.

There was no sign of any reversal in the decline of the blown glass industry, of which there had been eloquent indications in the second half of the eighteenth century. Apart from some isolated examples, the only activity on the island throughout the first half of the nineteenth century was the production of pearls, also known as 'glass beads'.

In the years following Austria's annexation of the Veneto (1815), there was not only an expansion of Bohemian products on all markets, but also an increase in the tariffs on imports of raw materials and exports of finished product, as a result of the policy followed by the Habsburg Empire to the total disadvantage of Lombardy-Veneto. In 1820 the number of Murano glass works producing blown glass had fallen to only five. Although disheartened and reduced to almost nothing by the distressing circumstances, the art of blown glass continued all the same to have a few resolute and impassioned adherents on the island, who treasured the past traditions.

At the exhibitions between 1825 and 1846 in Venice and Vienna, the names of Pietro Bigaglia, Domenico Busssolin and Lorenzo Radi frequently reappear among the prize-winners. They must also be merited with having actively contributed to the rebirth of blown glass.

It was a Venetian antiques dealer, Antonio Sanquirico, who urged those few masters still capable of exercising their craft to take a backward look at the works of past centuries. He had them reproduce antique examples in *retortoli* glass and sold them as originals.

[52.]

Although the fraud was discovered, that type of glass took on the name *zanfirico*, the dialect form of Sanquirico, by which it is still known today.
At the same time Domenico Bussolin had successfully resumed production of filigree in 1838. This technique was imitated a few years later, in 1845, by Pietro Bigaglia, who applied it to a vast number of pieces, many of which he personally donated to the museum in 1861. They included vases, beakers, fruit stands, candlesticks, cups and plates in a vibrantly coloured glass with interwoven rods of every colour, including aventurine, which, forgotten since the end of the eighteenth century, he brought back to life.
The shapes of his work, always linear and of great solidity, were in perfect harmony with the Biedermeier style that was so popular in Venice at the time. The only blemish is the excessive sobriety of his creations on a formal level, but they are technically impeccable (52, 54).
Bigaglia's example was followed by Lorenzo Graziati, a master who,

53. Lorenzo Graziati, bottle in milk glass and turquoise reticello *work, c. 1850.*

54. Pietro Bigaglia, bottle in polychrome filigree, c. 1846.

55. Lorenzo Radi, jug in glass imitating chalcedony, 1856.

[53.]

between 1850 and 1860, worked with great accuracy, as can be seen by the precision of his filigree work (53).
The main interest of the glass-makers of these years was the study and rediscovery of the inventions of previous centuries whose recipes had been lost.
Lorenzo Radi, who had formulated coloured gold leaf pastes for mosaics, following extensive studies carried out with Francesco Torcellan, managed to once again produce chalcedony glass, using the same composition as that of the fifteenth century. He presented some examples of his work to the Regio Istituto di Scienze, Lettere e Arti and, although awarded a silver medal, did not win great public success.
A considerable quantity of his chalcedony is now in the Glass Museum, donated by Radi himself in 1861. The pieces are mainly simple, linear forms, in some cases enlivened by bulges on the neck or foot of some pieces, or by grinding work, as on the hexagonal bowl of a goblet. Every effect was achieved with the vitreous substance in gob-

[54.] [55.]

[56.]

lets, glasses, cups and jars of every kind, marked by a vast range of veining from green to brown and red, at times with inclusions of aventurine, as in the bottle with lobed body (55). They are generally smallish objects, but the glass-maker's skill at making quite large works is also recalled, including 'a gigantic chandelier.'

Some years later, between 1880 and 1890, the same kind of glass was also made by another studio, the Francesco Ferro & Figlio, whose work could easily be mistaken for that of Radi, if its origin was not specifically known.

The first signs of a positive change for Murano became apparent in 1854 when the F.lli Toso glass works started operations. It initially specialised in the production of everyday glass, but after a few years also began making art glass in antique style that won unconditional approval, such as to be awarded the gold medal at the First and Second Murano Glass Exhibitions in 1864 and 1869. A few years later, in 1859, a Vicenza solicitor, Antonio Salviati, set up a mosaic art workshop in Venice in association with Lorenzo Radi.

Finally, in 1861, the first nucleus was formed of the future Glass

[59.]

[58.]

56. F.lli Toso, big goblet with lid and stem decorated with an elaborate rosette, c. 1864.

57. F.lli Toso, big lattice goblet with opaline glass goslings, c. 1867.

58. Salviati & C., goblet with stem in the form of a snake, c. 1877.

59. F.lli Toso, big goblet with twisted column stem, c. 1867.

60. Salviati & C., tureen in turquoise vitreous paste with milk glass flower handle, c. 1867.

61. Salviati & C., mosque lamp in polychrome enamels and gold by Leopoldo Bearzotti, 1869.

Museum, which was to have also played a promotional role on the island, providing young glass-makers attending the associated design school with stimuli and incentives to match and possibly surpass the excellent products of antiquity. In those years the museum played a guiding role in reviving the styles, techniques and manual skills that had distinguished the masters of the past but had more or less fallen into oblivion in the last fifty years, due to the difficult political and economic situation.
The Veneto's union with Italy in 1866, and subsequent political and economic changes, contributed to the recovery of industry and that of Murano in particular.
It was in that same year that Antonio Salviati decided to set up a glass-blowing furnace in Murano, mainly because he was favourably struck by the enthusiasm for Murano glass in London; indeed, the Società Anonima per Azioni Salviati & C. was founded

[60.]

with a contribution of English capital. The glass-makers put themselves to the test with very complex pieces intended to show off their regained skills, also on a manual level, and to show that the great traditions of the island were still alive.

[61.]

This is demonstrated in the beautiful goblet with lid of considerable height made by F.lli Toso around 1864, distinguished by a stem with cluster of flowers inscribed in a *morise* decorated circle.
The difficulty of the blowing is complemented by the free-hand crafting in the rosette and the hot applications on the stem (56).
Two works from 1867 are eloquent examples of the levels of expertise reached in the course of a few years by the company's glass-makers: the big pink, reticulated goblet decorated at the top of each lozenge with milk glass flowers and with dragons on the stem and lid; and the other, with big pediment, which within the complex net, all created free-hand, encloses goslings in opaline glass within archlets (57).
Dexterity, speed, precision and safety, accompanied by the desire to succeed at increasingly arduous tests of prowess, were needed to make the tall goblet with wavy edged cup and, on the stem, a big rosette crowned by flowers at the centre of which rests a gosling; and the one supported by pretty, twisted columns, which also decorate the lid (59).
A year after opening, Antonio Salviati's workshop also achieved exceptional results, presenting more than 500 different glass objects at the Universal Exhibition of Paris (1867). These were intended as a reinterpretation of those of the sixteenth century, but clearly embodied the eclectic style of the age. They were all sold and heralded the company's triumph.
Salviati's lively business is documented by the elegant tureen in turquoise vitreous paste. The uniformity of its very bright colour is broken by the charming detail of the handle on the lid in the shape of a flower in white and yellow paste (1867 c.) (60).
But it was in the goblets that the imagination of Salviati's master glass-makers seemed to know no bounds. The bowls, in the most diverse shapes and sizes, are supported by stems with animals, flowers, or even in the form of snakes, in imitation of the items made *à la façon de Venise* that were so popular in the Netherlands in the seventeenth century (58).

Decoration with fusible polychrome enamels was an integral part of the Murano tradition being revived. The painter Giuseppe Devers had considerable experience working with enamelled ceramics and was employed by Salviati immediately after the Paris exhibition.
At the Second Murano Glass Exhibition in 1869, the Salviati glass works presented a range of mosque lamps ordered by the viceroy of Egypt, very similar to the one in the museum. The glass for these was blown by Antonio Seguso, the enamels cast by Antonio Tosi and they were decorated by Leopoldo Bearzotti, who had studied under Devers (61). This was proof that the ancient methods of the island could still be revived.
The expertise of the glass-makers was put to a further test in 1875 when the dealer Michelangelo Guggenheim wanted some period glass items reproduced. They included a complicated cup that attracted attention because of the relative difficulty of its production.

62. Vincenzo Moretti, Compagnia di Venezia e Murano, vase and skyphos in murrine *glass, 1878.*

63. Vincenzo Moretti, Compagnia di Venezia e Murano, bowl in mosaic glass with flowers, birds and butterflies, c. 1880.

[62.]

The best master craftsmen of the time took up the challenge, which led to the object being successfully made by the leading workshops. The big cup, whose stem and lid handle are made up of *perloni* and small bridges in crystal and blue glass, was from then on known as a 'Guggenheim'. There are various versions, because it became part of the range offered both by the Compagnia di Venezia e Murano, a company that had taken over the Società Anonima Salviati in 1872; and F.lli Toso, which presented variants between 1875 and 1880, in which the stem and the top of the lid have a no less complicated application of blue filaments in place of the small chains.

[63.]

The separation of Salviati from the Compagnia di Venezia e Murano in 1877 led to the foundation of two new companies: Salviati & C. for working mosaics, and Salviati Dr. Antonio for blowing glass. The separation took place just before the Universal Exhibition of Paris (1878), where both the Compagnia and Salviati presented very similar collections, having not been able to create works that would show off their distinctive styles.

This makes the certain attribution of some works difficult, such as the tall goblet with rosette in blue glass and milk glass flowers, the one with the squashed bubble stem and the flute in very fine glass, that could all be attributed to either of the firms.

The novelty at the Paris exhibition was in any case mosaic glass, also known as *millefiori* or *murrini*, a term that had been borrowed, incorrectly interpreted, from Pliny's *Naturalis Historia*, where 'vasa myrrhina' indicated a jar made by carving fluorspar. In addition to recovering their past, the glass-makers also made a careful study of antique glass, specifically that consisting of sections of polychrome and gilt vitreous rods and strips joined by heat. Glass of this type gained popularity around 1870, when the first attempts were made to reproduce it.

Mosaic glass consists of numerous sections of *millefeuille* canes, joined by heating and worked either by blowing or shaping in moulds. In this case, too, the making of the cane is essential. In section it has a decoration, usually geometrical or floral, obtained by the overlapping of various layers of colour, some of which are given a clearly defined shape by placing them in different moulds.

The *murrine* can be used both to decorate a blown glass item and to create a piece made in a mould.

In the first case the sections of cane are arranged, on an iron plate at times forming a prepared design. The plate is heated in the furnace and removed now and then so that the *murrine* can be compacted using iron bars to ensure there are no spaces between one and the other. In the meantime, a certain quantity of glass has been taken from the pot with the blowpipe, which is blown until it opens. A ring known as a *mocaura* is then made by repeatedly placing it in the furnace and over the *bronzin*. The circumference of the ring must be the same as the length of the mat of *murrine* on the plate. A cylinder is obtained by rolling the *mocaura* on the base of the mat of *murrine* arranged on the plate, which is closed at the open end by being reheated and placed over the *bronzin* with the *tagiante tonda*, as for filigree. The closed, reheated cylinder is subject to light blowing to check that there are no gaps between one murrina and another. The subsequent stages of the work proceed with blowing and shaping by hand, for which various tools are used depending on the type of object being made.

In the case of *murrine* used for an object that requires the use of a mould, mainly bowls and plates, they are arranged on the plate so as to form a circular surface. They are welded together by heating in

[64.]

the furnace on the plate, after any gaps between the individual *murrine* have been filled with bits of vitreous cane and, once the plate has been taken out of the furnace, will be compacted with suitably shaped pincers. The resulting disc is placed hot on a previously heated kind of refractory and again placed in the furnace where it softens and assumes the desired shape. After cooling the object is ground and polished or subject to other treatments.
Vincenzo Moretti (1835-1901) devoted himself to this technique more than anyone else. He worked first for the Società Anonima per Azioni Salviati & C. preparing the vitreous pastes, before moving to the Compagnia di Venezia e Murano.
This workshop produced the most perfect examples of mosaic glass in the nineteenth century.
It attracted great admiration when exhibited in Paris at the Universal Exhibition (1878) and in 1879 Moretti even went to Naples to examine the antique mosaic glass held at the Archaeological Museum there, with the aim of equalling its perfection of workmanship. A few years later the Compagnia di Venezia e Murano donated some

64. Vincenzo Moretti, Compagnia di Venezia e Murano, large plate in mosaic glass with floral motifs, 1879-1883.

65. Giuseppe Barovier, Salviati Dr. Antonio, plate in blue mosaic glass with floral motifs, 1881.

[65.]

[66.]

of these to the Murano Museum, where they are still held. They include a big truncated conical jar with lid in a glass consisting of green, white and amber spiral weaves, and a bowl in the shape of a *skyphos*, with polychrome bands and undulating gold leaf, polished at the wheel and edged with a twisted brown and opaline cane; it was made for the Paris exhibition and was a copy of a Hellenistic original (62).

A great variety of precious, refined glass materials makes up the vast range of Vincenzo Moretti's work, including flowers, birds and butterflies of rare elegance, such as the white bowl (63) or, more simply, materials of various colours such as that with irregular white and

66. *Artisti Barovier, cup with spiral stem, 1895.*

67. *F.lli Toso, flower goblet, c. 1900.*

amethyst fragments on a blue base. The most beautiful examples of this production, from around the 1880s, include the turquoise plate made up of tesserae of a rich polychrome with floral motifs of very modern stylisation, and the black plate, exemplary not only for the singularity of its dimensions, but also for the great variety of floral motifs that give it the resemblance of a fascinating Oriental carpet (64).

The fashion for mosaic glass was quickly taken up by all the studios on the island and, as well as the F.lli Toso, Salviati Dr. Antonio was also much involved in this sector. An example of its work is a blue plate made by Giuseppe Barovier around 1881, featuring a rich sample of floral *murrine* with the poetic naive style in their almost abstract geometrical appearance (65).

[67.]

Francesco Toso, called Borella, interpreted the centuries-old tradition of fusible polychrome enamel decoration with great technical skill and singular sensitivity in the last two decades of the century. Two fine amethyst glass cups with elaborate ornamentation framing scenes inspired by the classical world by him are signed FTB.

The intense activity in Murano in the second half of the nineteenth century was mainly related to reviewing and reviving the past, leaving the island culturally isolated from the rest of Europe and the USA. In the 1890s Art Nouveau was in full swing elsewhere and classical models were being abandoned. Normal production in Murano was still that of the nineteenth century, with its abundant decoration. The glass-makers remained technically and stylistically anchored to their past and not even the first Venice Biennale of 1895 inspired any updating.

An *Exhibition of selected art glass and fine objects from Murano and Venice* was organised in Murano to coincide with the Biennale. This was very successful, but the only modern works were some pieces by the Artisti Barovier, noted as being 'the acme of audacity for their fineness and lightness,' but not part of the competition.

One of these, the spiral cup, was donated to the museum by the Artisti Barovier the following year. The very simple but quite sophisticated structure consists of a foot and enlarged cone bowl connected by a spiral of glass of considerable elasticity, making it

quite different from the highly elaborate constructions that were typical of the island's masters (66).
So Murano began the twentieth century completely in line with tradition. In the early years mosaic glass continued to be highly successful and for some years was to remain a cornerstone for the leading glass works: the Compagnia di Venezia e Murano, Salviati & C. and F.lli Toso.
A first, timid, opening up to Art Nouveau was made in the fine, flower-shaped goblet whose corolla opens up on a stem enriched with leaves. This was made by F.lli Toso around 1900, as documented by drawings of the period (67).
The numerous vases that appear in the company's catalogues also refer to the floral style, although applied in the literal sense of the term. They are exemplified by those in the Glass Museum, made with polychrome tesserae with flowers, arranged one beside the other in a lively assortment of colours (69).
Attention was also focused on pre-Roman glassware with a friable core, at the time known as *fenici* (Phoenician glass), which was reproduced with a completely different procedure than that used in

[68.]

antiquity. Rather than wrapping vitreous filaments around a friable core, which was subsequently eliminated, the glass-makers used to blow the glass, imitating the shapes and decoration of the threads in the originals, in this case applied hot. The most successful 'Phoenician' glass include the very interesting examples in the museum's collection documenting the work of F.lli Toso between 1900 and 1915.

The difficulty of freeing themselves from the historic styles and the cultural isolation of the island was not only evident at the Universal Exhibition of Paris in 1900 and that of Decorative Arts in Turin in 1902, but also in the Milan exhibition of 1906, where the only Murano glass-maker who seemed to have taken in the floral style with any real sensitivity was the decorator Francesco Toso Borella, son of Vittorio, who had learnt the craft from his father. Although the decorated glass objects presented by the artist in Milan were lost in the fire that destroyed the Italian and Hungarian pavilions, the direction of his style was clarified in the years immediately after by the works he presented in Venice at the second Permanent Ca' Pesaro Exhibition (1909). The critics emphasised the innovative nature of

[69.]

68. Vittorio Toso Borella, bowl and vase decorated with opaque enamels showing nymphs and herons, c. 1909.

69. F.lli Toso, floral murrine *jug, c. 1910.*

his works, 'some reproducing classical objects, others adorned with modern decorations [...] treated with original spirit, with an aristocratic sense of art, to which the critics and public devoted [...] the most attention and the most unconditional praise'.

The bowl and jar in the museum dating from between 1906 and 1909 belong to this category. They are decorated with transparent opaque enamels, one with fine nymphs and the other with herons in flight, which were quite new subjects in the island's repertoire (68).

Mosaic glass remained the centre of attention for most serious glass-makers in Murano during the first twenty years of the new century. Exceptional examples of this were presented by the Artisti Barovier at the Ca' Pesaro exhibition of 1913, where the *Murrina del pavone* appeared, now in the museum. It was made by Giuseppe Barovier, considered a genuine 'wizard of glass art'. The section of cane, in reduced dimensions, has the multi-coloured image of a peacock with its long, flowing tail (70).

The dynamic relationship between the Artisti Barovier and the painter Vittorio Zecchin, also from Murano, was probably formed

70. Giuseppe Barovier, Murrina del pavone *(Peacock* murrine*), 1913.*

71. Vittorio Zecchin - Artisti Barovier, Barbaro *plate, 1914.*

72. Hans Stoltenberg Lerche, F.lli Toso, vase in applied filaments, 1911.

[70.]

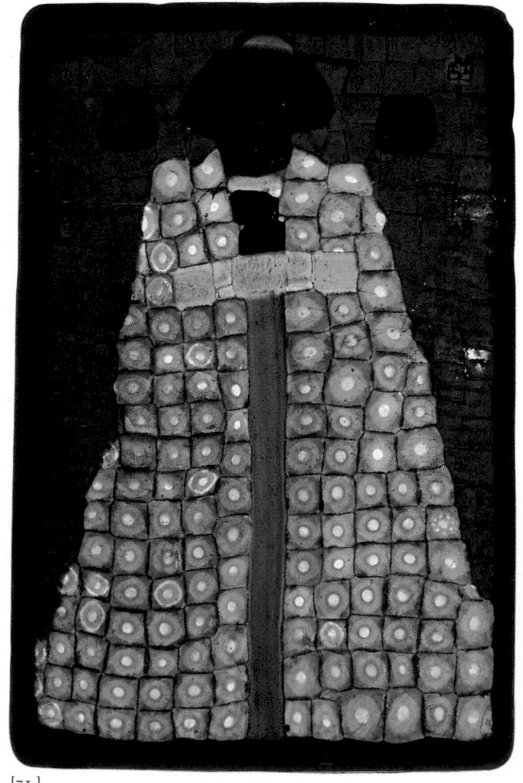

[71.]

[72.]

thanks to their appearances at Ca' Pesaro. Zecchin was heavily influenced by the elegant and linear stylisations of Jan Toorop, who had been present at the 1905 Biennale, to which he later added the rich and precious palette suggested by Klimt at the 1910 Biennale. Linearity, rarefied elegance and intense colour are the distinctive marks of the artist's creations made by Artisti Barovier in glass, to which he devoted a large part of his work, though without neglecting other sectors of applied arts, such as embroidery and tapestry. A series of plates in mosaic glass appeared at the 1914 Biennale, including the very famous *Barbaro* and the very expressive one with a highly stylised female face, in which the influence of Klimt is evident, made by the Artisti Barovier (71).

The other important studio assiduously involved in making mosaic glass was F.lli Toso, which was very open to innovative ferments and stimuli.

The association with the artist Hans Stoltenberg Lerche, which gave rise to very modern vases creating vitreous materials quite uncommon for Murano, was particularly productive in this sense, though it remained an isolated incident of the period. The fine vase with applied polychrome filaments, similar to seaweed, is from 1911, as shown in a photograph signed and dated by Lerche himself (72).

Mosaic glass was often associated with objects in wrought iron made by Umberto Bellotto in the 1920s. He was the son of a blacksmith and had opened a wrought iron workshop in Venice, noted by the writings of the time as 'the workshop of the wizard.'

Fascinated by glass, mainly using the F.lli Toso furnace, he made it the natural partner of his elaborate supports in wrought iron. At the 1914 Biennale he appeared with what were defined as 'marriages of iron and glass.' Bellotto exhibited at the first postwar Biennale of 1920 with works of this kind, and at that of 1924 an individual exhibition was devoted to his work.

His most significant works date from these years. A very elegant oval vase rests on a slender base in wrought iron with a figurine crouching to support the two big handles. It is an extremely successful work in mosaic glass with transparent tesserae that form a material of a light green enhanced by flashes from the gold leaf on which, in the middle of luxuriant vegetation, the figure of a stylised peacock is set.

The skill of craftsmanship could suggest the work of the F.lli Toso studio, while the elegance of the subject would make the participation of Vittorio Zecchin quite likely. An openly celebratory function may be associated with the other work by the artist dedicated to Giovanni Giuriati, signed and dated 1919-1923. It is a bowl studded with floral mosaic glass, probably made by F.lli Toso, resting on a crown of laurels held up by a stem whose decorative elements, along with the crown, symbolically allude to the role Giuriati had had in Italian politics regarding the Adriatic question and the events in Fiume (Rijeka) in 1919, where he had been D'Annunzio's parliamentary private secretary (73). It was no mere chance that this tribute to the politician had been commissioned from Bellotto, as Giuriati was a great connoisseur of the artist's work, such that, when he took over the Public Works portfolio in 1925, he assigned demanding projects to the person he had defined as a 'illustrious tamer of iron' that put an end to his interest in glass.

[73.]

73. Umberto Bellotto - F.lli Toso (?), Giuriati Cup *in mosaic glass with floral decoration on a complex wrought iron support with a symbolic character, c. 1923*

The 1920s were marked by innovation and change, especially in the formal aspect of production in Murano, after a period of stagnation caused by the war. The models inspired by Art Nouveau and the floral style were gradually abandoned before an opening up to the functionalism and essentiality propounded from 1907 by Deutscher Werkbund, with all useless decorative elements forbidden. A fundamental guiding role was taken on in this context by a new company, Vetri Soffiati Muranesi Cappellin Venini & C., which had been set up in 1921 by a Venetian antiques dealer moved to Milan, Giacomo Cappellin, a young Milan solicitor, Paolo Venini, who at first took charge of the administrative-promotional aspect, and the well-known designer Vittorio Zecchin as art director.
The presence of an art director with responsibility for giving production a precise stylistic direction that would allow immediate identification of the work was an absolute innovation of this century, and was to be quickly taken up by other companies on the island. The abolition of every decorative element distinguished the creations of Vittorio Zecchin, who began making a review of the pure forms of sixteenth-century glass, often taken from Renaissance paintings, such as the 'Veronese' jar, which appears in Paolo Veronese's *Annunciation*, now in the Venice Accademia, or the big goblet whose sides are marked with light ribbing. The use of light, absolutely transparent colours, such as pale green, aquamarine, straw-yellow and amethyst, are typical of those years and distin-

[74.]

[75.]

74. VSM Cappellin Venini & C., goblets in very fine glass, 1921 - 1925.

75. VSM Cappellin Venini & C., hexagonal bottle and glasses in very fine glass, 1921-1925.

guish all the examples of the company's catalogue. The same purity of line, with a very light, sharp, crystalline material can be seen in the table services: the hexagonal glasses and bottles, whose form shows the influence of Art Deco (75), or the carafe, the bottle and the goblets with stems, taking up the Renaissance baluster, with a note, however, of absolute modernity in the light blue ring marking the join of the bowl to its support (1921- 1925) (74).
The company's production had great success at the Universal Exhibition of Paris in 1925, the same year the company was wound up, giving rise to two distinct firms: the Maestri Vetrai Muranesi Cappellin & C., to which Vittorio Zecchin remained associated, and Vetri Soffiati Muranesi Venini & C., whose art director was the sculptor Napoleone Martinuzzi. Zecchin soon decided to work as an independent designer and was replaced by the young architect Carlo Scarpa. After his debut with soft, rounded silhouettes in very thin, transparent glass, in keeping with the island's traditions, he showed off his preference for simple forms of a pure geometry but accompanied by a precious material, carefully studied in its compo-

76. Carlo Scarpa - MVM Cappellin & C., carafe in red vitreous paste with gold leaf, c. 1930.

77. Napoleone Martinuzzi - VSM Venini & C., cactus in pulegoso *glass, 1926-1930.*

[76.]

[77.]

78. Napoleone Martinuzzi - VSM Venini & C., vase with nine spouts in green pulegoso *glass, 1930.*

79. Carlo Scarpa (?) - MVM Cappelin & C., octopus in green glass with murrine *eyes, 1930-1931.*

[78.]

[79.]

sition, as seen in the carafe in red vitreous paste enlivened by gleams from the gold leaf (1930 c.) (76).
At the time of the separation from Cappellin, Paolo Venini found himself in the position of having to create his company's production line from the start. He was greatly aided in this by Martinuzzi, who quickly launched the company's collection with a completely new approach. He replaced the transparent and very light blown objects with volumes of definite plastic character that fully reflected his background in sculpture, and gradually abandoned Art Deco styles in favour of the Novecento style.
The move is already apparent in the filigree and bubble glass ducklings from the 1928 Biennale, which nevertheless still retain some mannerisms of the past. But it was to become quite evident in subsequent years when the volumetric effects were reinforced by the use of a thick, opaque glass, sprinkled with bubbles and for this reason known as *pulegoso* (from *pulega*, bubble, in the language of the

[80.]

[81.]

glass-makers); it was to be used for numerous creations. Martinuzzi's imagination ranged from cacti, some of considerable size, to various animals and vases. In addition to the ducklings in filigree and bubble glass (1926-1928), the museum collection includes imaginary animals like the unicorn, a cactus in green *pulegoso* (77), a jar with nine spouts (78) and another decorated with heavy stripes, as well as a varied series of fruit, vegetables and trees that had never previously attracted the attention of the glass world.
They were absolutely new shapes with no precedent, usually made with non-transparent glass, plastically shaped but nevertheless blown. In the end heavy, opaque glass had such vast application that most Murano glass works adopted it for small animals in the round. A charming bestiary was also created by the Cappellin company: the most handsome animals were perhaps the elephants, always shown in positions of great movement, but the vibrant octopus in pale green glass (1930-1931) is inimitable. Its big eyes are made from two *murrine* the same as those Carlo Scarpa had used in some of his jars, so it is not unlikely that the work of the architect may also be identified in this work (79).
After working with Stoltenberg Lerche, F.lli Toso engaged the services of the painter Guido Cadorin on the occasion of the Decorative Arts Exhibition of Monza in 1923. Cadorin conceived of glass as the decorative complement of a living room with painted furniture and fabrics by the Venetian Rubelli company. The big compote with lid

80. Vittorio Zecchin - AVEM, goblets in crystal and smoky glass with blown stem, 1932.

81. Vittorio Zecchin - F.lli Toso, goblets with leaf, 1938.

82. Guido Balsamo Stella S.A.L.I.R., amphora with wheel engraved Leda and the Swan, *1927-1930.*

[82.]

[83.]

83. Alfredo Barbini - VAMSA, coot in hot shaped solid glass, 1938-1940.

84. Giulio Radi - AVEM, polychrome reaction plate, 1952.

decorated with a bunch of lemons is preserved; the basically linear form is enriched by vitreous threads worked with pincers and seems, in those years, an ironic look back at Murano's eighteenth-century production.

After leaving the Cappellin company, Vittorio Zecchin certainly did not abandon glass, despite his broad interests in the field of applied arts. The goblets designed with a rigorous geometrism, in keeping with the furniture of the time and whose stem is also blown, date from 1932; they were made by AVEM, one of the emerging studios of those years (80).

The artist subsequently (1938) reasserted his interest in table furnishings, conceiving other very elegant goblets for F.lli Toso, with the bowl slightly opening into a corolla and the very fine and quite tall stem decorated with leaflets, that were much admired in the company's showcase at the 21st Venice Biennale (81). Some very skilled experts in wheel engraved decoration were employed by the S.A.L.I.R. workshop in the second decade of the century. The com-

[84.]

pany had been set up in 1923 and boasted the services of the etcher Guido Balsamo Stella as designer and the Bohemian engraver Franz Pelzel, who would teach the younger generations in Murano. The workshops' vases, usually in linear, classical form, were engraved with a great variety of subjects, from typically Venetian scenes to mythological figures and representations of contemporary life open to the suggestions of Futurism. The masterfully applied engraving, with great plastic and representative effect, appears in the jar with a squashed body decorated with the images of *Leda and the Swan*, designed both in form and subject by Balsamo Stella and engraved by Pelzel between 1927 and 1930 (82).
S.A.L.I.R. also occasionally employed other artists as designers. Among these was Vittorio Zecchin who, continuing in his direction of purity and formal severity, in 1934 conceived designs based predominantly on nature for thick vases on a heavy hammered base, such as the very elegant one with vegetable decorations spread over its entire surface.

In the second half of the 1930s, in keeping with current styles, a positive eye was cast toward heavy glass. This had previously not been considered authentic Murano glass, because it was blown and worked manually. One of those who unconditionally accepted it, however, in virtue of its plastic properties, was Alfredo Barbini. As a partner in VAMSA (Vetri Artistici Muranesi Società per Azioni), founded in 1937, he created some genuine small sculptures between 1938 and 1940 including heads, nudes and birds, such as the fine coot and owl in solid glass, submerged and shaped hot (83). Barbini's preference for heavy glass was to continue when he opened his own glass works in 1950, the same year the small sculpture of the *Nudo al sole* was made. After the forced period of inactivity during the second world war, the glass works returned to business with renewed vigour, focusing particular attention on heavy glass, though without ignoring the light version, with all its traditional techniques and fascinating chromatic effects. The 'polychrome reaction' glass conceived by Giulio Radi for AVEM between 1950 and 1952 was a

85. Fulvio Bianconi - Venini & C., bottles with polychrome bands, 1952-1956.

86. Flavio Poli - Seguso Vetri d'Arte, Valva *in submerged glass, 1954.*

87. Flavio Poli - Seguso Vetri d'Arte, vase in violet submerged glass, 1954.

[85.]

very interesting example of non-transparent heavy glass objects with special colourings. They are exemplified by two vases and a plate that, in their simple formal elegance, highlight the polychrome vitreous material with gold leaf using quite new chromatic effects, obtained using new reactions of metallic colouring agents (84). The sculptor Napoleone Martinuzzi, after working with Paolo Venini, turned again to very evocative figurative works of great emotional impact in the '50s with a kind of particularly rough surfaced glass, for this reason called 'corrugated'. These included the two big heads made with Alberto Toso's Arte Vetro glass works, which were presented at the Milan Triennale (1951) and the Venice Biennale the following year.

Flavio Poli, one of the most interesting designers working in Murano, devoted himself almost exclusively to 'submerged' heavy glass, in which several layers of different colour are overlapped. He worked with Barovier Seguso & Ferro from the '30s, then with Seguso Vetri d'Arte where he became a partner in 1937. The artist con-

[86.]

[87.]

[88.]

ceived animals and vases of a very pure line, in which the overlapping, differently coloured, vitreous layers allowed a sequential reading of the clear profiles of the object. Poli's work is well represented in the museum's collections. Alongside the *Valva* of 1954 (86), which quickly became a classic of twentieth-century Murano glass, the vases are quite indicative, always in very sober, essential form, among which is the ruby, blue and violet one that won the 'Compasso d'Oro' award in the same year (87). The pieces with 'submerged' glass are studies he continued over the years with very significant formal results, such as those of 1962.
Paolo Venini's glass works was also distinguished by some very intriguing activity in the 1950s. It worked not so much with heavy glass as in the recovery and re-presentation of traditional Murano techniques. Numerous people contributed to this as designers, though always under the direction of Paolo Venini with his sure taste and infallible instincts. He personally created glass items of lasting success, too, such that they are still being reproduced today.
Fulvio Bianconi took over from Carlo Scarpa as artistic director, and in 1948-1949 with Venini conceived one of the pieces that became a kind of symbol for the company: the *Fazzoletto*. It was inspired by one designed by Pietro Chiesa for Fontana Arte in 1936 but made by moulding. This version was blown and worked by hand, with the application of typically Murano techniques, from cane glass to half filigree and *zanfirico*, like the example in the museum. It was to be

widely copied by all the glass works on the island and destined to remain in the company's catalogue due to its success. Examples from the 1950s include the elegant vase with vertical polychrome stripes and the bottles with uneven horizontal bands, with impressive cap, designed by Fulvio Bianconi and presented at the 1956 Biennale (85); and the more geometrical ones whose surface is concealed by a fairly dense series of light engravings, and thus called *incise* (engraved), conceived by Paolo Venini. The same decorative technique was to reappear some years later on big vases with a rounded profile in charming colours.
The company was taken over by Paolo Venini's son-in-law, the architect Ludovico Diaz de Santillana, after Venini's death in 1959, and in the '60s continued producing work of excellent quality. The *Colletti* vases with their simple lines in fine, blown glass, distinguished by the neck in a different colour applied with the difficult *incalmo* tech-

88. Ludovico de Santillana - Venini & C., Colletti *vases, 1961.*

89. Barbara Del Vicario - Venini SpA, Fiamma *vase, 1986.*

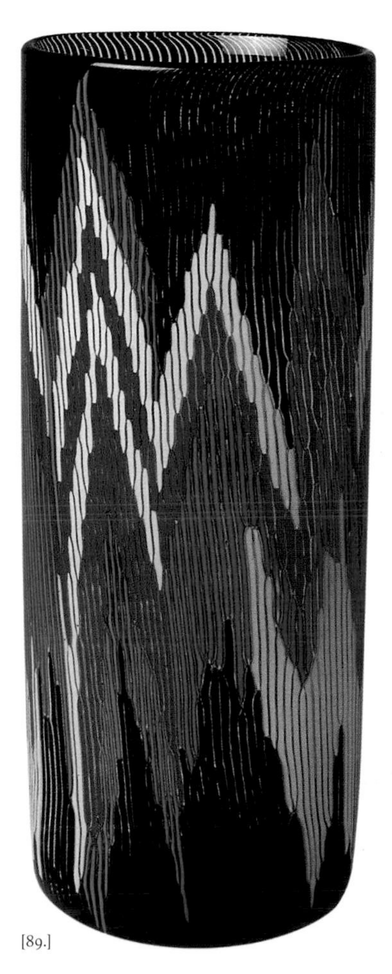

[89.]

90. Laura de Santillana – Venini & C., Mimosa *plate in* murrine *glass, 1977.*

91. Laura de Santillana - Venini & C., Klee *vase, 1978.*

nique, are from 1961 and were designed by De Santillana (88). Among the numerous artists who worked for the studio, Toni Zuccheri made a big contribution to updating the catalogue with his extraordinary bestiary, which included the hoopoe and guinea fowl presented at the 1964 Biennale. The artist's poetic interpretations of the animal world were created with the most elaborate techniques, from hot shaping to mosaic glass blowing, through to solid ground polychrome glass for the duck, of which the museum has an example from 1978.

In more recent years (1986), Barbara Del Vicario emerged as a very sensitive interpreter of cane glass, with a very personal compositional style and refined sense of colour. She created the *Fiamma* vase, consisting of a series of thin canes of various size arranged to represent a flame and involving a fairly difficult technique (89).

Mosaic glass continued to appear in Venini's work over the years, giving rise to the original compositions of Laura de Santillana at the end of the '70s. The *Mimosa* plate (1977), with small sections of yellow rod concealed by expert use of the grindstone (90), is particularly successful. Then, the following year, the artist's desire to try out the most diverse techniques inspired her to make the sophisticated *Klee* vase, consisting of diagonal tesserae of various colour on an inner layer of milk glass. The museum has the prototype of the series (91).

The Venini workshop was a markedly international environment to which artists and designers from all over the world came to test their skills. Among these, Tapio Wirkkala of Finland made a particular mark. He was already an established glass artist in his own country and immediately showed a comprehensive understanding not only of the techniques of Murano glass, but also the chromatic

[90.]

refinements of the island's traditions. He designed very elegant works of great formal constraint, such as the *Bolle* bottles, created in 1966 and of which the museum has a 1970 version. They are pieces consisting of two or even three sections of different colours that are joined using the *incalmo* technique. This requires absolute precision as it involves joining two or more sections, blown separately, that have to have exactly the same diameter and thickness at the joint.

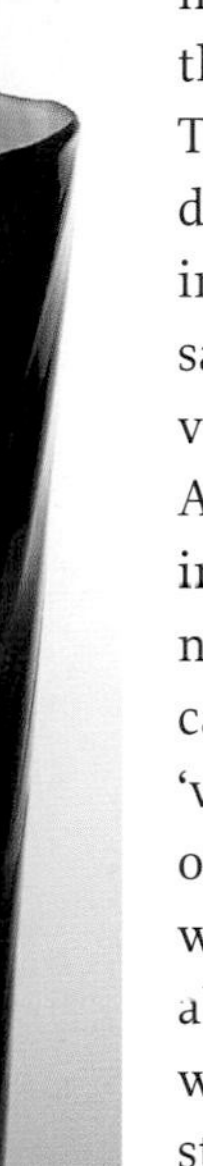

[91.]

The *Polipo* plate, with a delightful murrina depicting a small octopus at the centre, also inserted using the *incalmo* technique, is from the same year. Among the studios that focused innovatively on traditional techniques in the 1960s, Archimede Seguso had an important role working with thread glass. Apart from carrying out numerous experiments, creating fairly complicated weaves with filigree, the firm produced the 'vertical thread vases' in 1962. These were highly original not only in the unusual continuous white thread running from spout to base, but also because they were blown in a single piece in which the base is not applied nor created by constriction (92).

In the second half of the '80s, some of the more highly skilled masters in Murano no longer wished to be simply interpreters/makers of standard works, but to create and produce one-off pieces. The work of Lino Tagliapietra, currently one of the more sensitive interpreters of the island's traditions, is emblematic of the infinite expressive possibilities of blown and manually worked glass. He has offered proof of his exceptional skill, particularly in filigree, creating complex, new materials of an extremely graphic nature (93).

Giampaolo Martinuzzi has focused his attention on diamond engraving since the '70s, crowding blown pieces and thin plates with tiny, gaping figures. The artist, who has long since left the island to retire in Germany, always matched the glass with rough materials, often casually found items, such as wood and iron, on which time has left its indelible mark, as seen in the plate he donated to the museum (1980).

Salviati & C., whose artistic director had been the painter Luciano Gaspari from 1965, produced work of great elegance and simplicity in the years between the '70s and '80s. After a series of experiments with 'submerged' and mosaic glass, the artist turned his interest to very light blown glass, with which the 'bublle' vases a bolle were

[92.]

made, decorated at the base with a series of blown bubbles (1968), and, later, the *Zefiro* series of vases and bottles in sinuous forms, with a mark on the body that takes up the colour of the stopper (1982) (95).

The company's line of table services was directed by the architect Romano Chirivi with a great sense of proportion and function. He designed the *Acquamarina* and *Francesca* series in 1960 and, a few years later, gave a modern interpretation to the seventeenth-century *kuttrolf* tradition with the *Inutili* vases (94). Carlo Moretti dedicated his efforts to table services from the beginning of his career in 1970, then expanded his studies into purely decorative and lighting glass. The solutions he applied for services like the *Cartoccio*, the *Millemolature* and the *Petali* were particularly successful. They are marked by very elegant but audacious, unusual, innovative forms that stand alongside others more closely tied to tradition. In the last twenty years of the last century, collectors began to focus their attention on Murano glass products, especially those from the first half of the twentieth century, but then also on works from subsequent decades and through to the present.

92. Archimede Seguso, vertical thread vases, 1962.

93. Lino Tagliapietra e Maria Grazia Angelin - Effetre International, E *vase and* Orfeo *vase, 1984.*

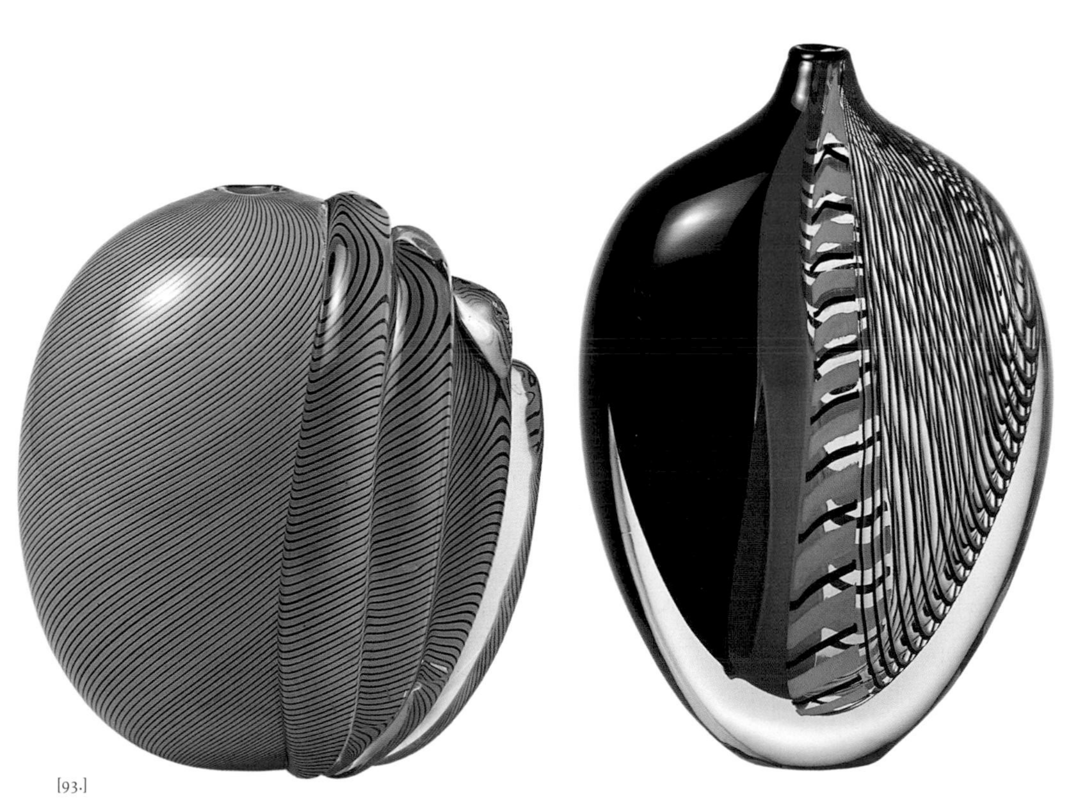

[93.]

One aspect of the Murano world has been the choice of numerous artists to use glass for their creations, especially in the last two decades. Some of them are wholly or partially involved in the actual production, others provide a detailed design and closely supervise the stages of its production by the master craftsman. Works by such artists are displayed in the big showcase on the end wall of the ticket sales and bookshop area on the ground floor, and in those of the nearby corridor.
One of the most assiduous visitors to Murano over the last ten years has been Yoichi Ohira, a Japanese artist (but now Venetian by adoption) of international renown. After working briefly with the De Majo company, he chose independence and now creates at least one collection per year of one-off examples that have been widely acclaimed by glass enthusiasts, who buy them through specialist galleries. The artist prefers mosaic glass for his work, allowing him to personally work on composing the glass tesserae and cane, which are then blown by the expert masters at the Anfora studio of Renzo Ferro, known for his particular openness to working with artists. Ohira has shown a rare sensitivity in managing to harmoniously

94. Romano Chirivi - Salviati & C., Inutili *vases, 1968.*

95. Luciano Gaspari - Salviati & C., Zefiro *vases, 1982.*

[94.]

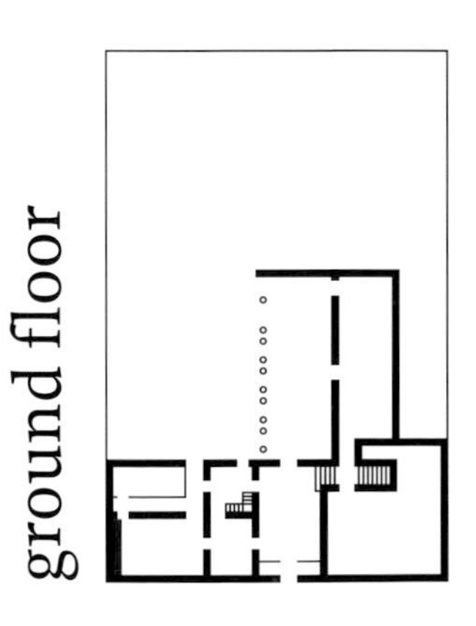

[95.]

96. Maria Grazia Rosin, Les Grandes Dames, *goblets with foot, 1999.*

97. Isabelle Poilprez, Fiore di Portland, *1999.*

98. Michele Burato, Tzigano *vase in mosaic glass, 1999.*

combine forms and colours of Oriental derivation with a purely Murano technique, though enhanced by his own inventions. He applies powders of contrasting colours and fascinating effects to opaque glass, then accentuates these by skilled grinding work, trying out all the possible contrasts between opacity and transparency. Such characteristics distinguish works like *Mosaico Blu*, *Polvere* with 'murrine' (101), *Finestre*, *Acqua Alta*, *Laguna* and *Silenzio*, made between 1997 and 1999, which the artist donated to the museum.
After her experience in painting, Maria Grazia Rosin began working with glass in 1992, producing works inspired by Pop Art and culminating in the *Detersivi* series. The artist quickly demonstrated her strong individuality: sensitivity, irony and contemplation of nature are brought together in the creation not only of the big chandeliers in the form of friendly tentacled octopuses, but also of goblets made up of elements of the female body and, not by chance, called *Les Grandes Dames* (1999) (96).
Cristiano Bianchin has carried out various experiments with glass since 1992, in which grinding and the multi-material nature of the compositions have an important role. Michele Burato creates high-

ly original materials with mosaic glass that are more in line with Murano traditions (98).

Isabelle Poilprez combines various materials taken directly from nature, such as dried flowers and shells, with the glass (97).

Finally, Massimo Nordio has carried out interesting experiments systematically focused on the study of technique and different materials from the Murano tradition (99).

Toni Zuccheri is still highly inventive. After his work with Venini, despite expressing his creativity in various other activities, he has never abandoned glass. It is an essential component of many multi-media works, such as the *Albero delle stagioni*, in the portico of the courtyard, and *Numina*: *Arcano*, a unique example in green blown glass with hot inclusions of aluminium (1998) (100), and *Cespuglio*, a composition in threads of iron, bronze and brass, on which a bird in blown glass, crystal and ruby with bronze feet stands. Among the

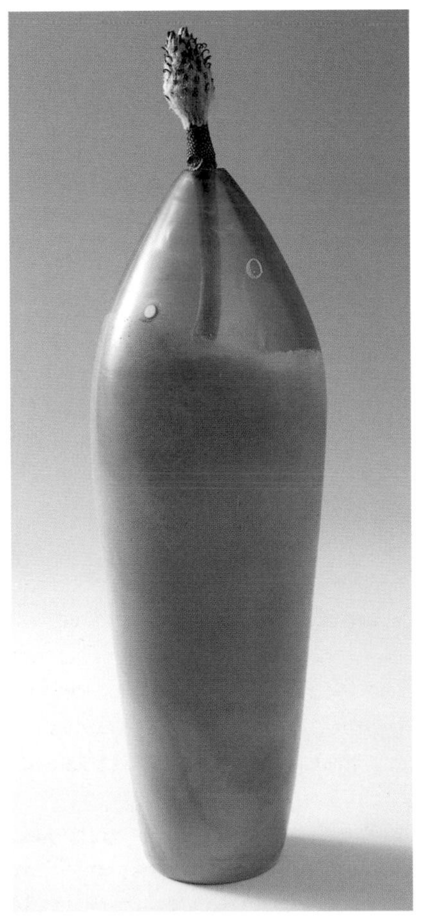

[97.]

[98.]

most striking contemporary works are those in the entrance to the museum and the garden. They were donated by the artists themselves or by the studios that produced them.

In the entrance there is a big vase with flowers: *Translucent Green Ikebana with Clear Flower* (1992), which one of the most renowned American glass artists, Dale Chihuly, creator and producer of the work, wanted to donate to the museum, mainly because his first experience with blown glass was in Murano, at the end of the 1960s, at Paolo Venini's workshop.

The *Cannucce* composition (1999) (103) is by Piero Lunetta, who is one of Murano's more promising young artists but does not devote himself exclusively to glass. It is made up of bases in solid, ground crystal onto which blown and bent canes are grafted, intended to hold big sunflowers in season.

[99.]

There are other important works in the garden: *Egg* (1998) (102), an ironic egg in blown glass with bronze feet, by Koen Vanmechelen of Holland, which was given to the museum by the workshop where it was made: Berengo Fine Arts; *Canneto*, a composition of elements in blown aventurine, by the sculptor Pino Castagna, who left it to the museum to document his work with glass; and *Enlightenments No.* 5 (2001), with elements in blown and ground glass supported by forged iron, donation of the artist Andrea Morucchio.

Many sculptural works from various places in Murano are also displayed in the garden and entrance. These were personally collected by Abbot Zanetti to document the island's important past, after tragic events had completely devastated not only its production, but also its urban order, particularly in the early nineteenth century.

The fine relief portraying *St John the Baptist consigning the gonfalon to the brothers of the Scuola di San Giovanni dei Battuti* dates from 1361. It was formerly in the Murano church of San Giovanni Battista dei Battuti, demolished in 1837. The fourteenth-century *Baptism of Christ*, at the top of the staircase leading to the first *piano nobile*, came from the same church. There are also numerous reliefs attached to the walls of the courtyard portico. They came from monasteries and churches that were closed as a result of the edicts of Napoleon and from demolished civil buildings, and are fairly indicative of Murano's opulent past. The sarcophagi and stone fragments dating from between the eighth and eleventh centuries are particularly interest-

99. Massimo Nordio, Luxor *vase in murrine, aventurine and polychrome canes, 1999.*

100. Toni Zuccheri, Numina *vase, 1998.*

101. Yoichi Ohira, Polvere *vase with* murrine, *1997.*

[100.]

[101.]

[102.]

ing. They were found during excavations carried out in the nearby church of Santi Maria e Donato in the second half of the nineteenth century to build the new sacristy and baptistery. The Byzantine sculptural decorations (ninth century) are of particular importance for the origins of Venetian sculpture; they were probably originally part of the ancient ciborium in the same church.
Finally, various well-heads may be seen both in the courtyard and garden, dating from between the fourteenth and fifteenth centuries. The one in Istrian stone with two lions of St Mark in *moleca* (dialect for crab), meaning in the form of a crab, between two crosses and hanging arches is particularly noteworthy, as is the one with human heads bearing the Murano coat of arms with the cockerel.

102. Koen Vanmechelen - Berengo Fine Arts, Egg, *installation in blown glass and bronze, 1998.*

103. Giampiero Lunetta, Cannucce, *installation with blown canes grafted onto bases in ground solid crystal, 1999.*

[103.]

Annealing furnace
Furnace in which the glass is placed after being worked to slowly cool

Aventurine
Cinnamon-yellow vitreous paste, distinguished by the presence in the mass of minuscule crystals of copper precipitated during the cooling of the cast. The name is derived from *ventura* (luck, fortune), and means that, even when carefully following all the prescribed technical steps, the result is not at all certain.

Baloton
Metal mould with its ends in the form of small pyramids with square base on the inside that give the glass a diamond decoration.

Blowpipe
Hollow iron pipe with one end slightly conical. It is used to take the glass from the pot and for blowing and moulding the object free-hand or in a mould.

Bole
Core of glass taken from the pot with the blowpipe from which, after being worked, the finished item will emerge. Also called *pea* or *posta.*

Borsella
Pincers of various size and shape used for specific operations of moulding, squeezing, cutting and decorating glass.

Bronzin
Iron plate, but once in marble or bronze, on whose surface the glass-maker rolls the bole to give it a cylindrical or pear shape. This operation is also called *marmorizar* (marbling).

Chalcedony glass
Opaque glass made by mixing silver salts and other colouring oxides into the cast in order to obtain a material similar to semi-precious stones like chalcedony, agate and malachite.

Calipers
Tool of various size consisting of two straight or curved rods, joined by a hinge, used to check the size of the object during its formation.

Cold painting
Follows the same procedure as enamel painting but does not involve any heat treatment, which is why the decorations often fade.

Enamel painting
Painting carried out with colorants mixed with powdered glass with greasy essences or substances; it is applied to the sides of the object which, reattached to the *pontello,* is returned to the mouth of the furnace at about 1000° C until the enamels adhere perfectly and become indelible. Also called fusible enamel painting.

Filigree
Decorative technique invented in the sixteenth century that involves the use of vitreous canes containing threads in milk glass or coloured glass. The *retortoli* or *retorti* version is distinguished by canes with threads woven in various ways, while in the *reticello* version, also known as double filigree, the threads of opaque glass cross to form diamonds similar to those of a mesh, with a small bubble of air trapped inside.

Frit
Partially vitrified spongy aggregate obtained by reheating the flux (ashes) and the vitrescible mixture (sand) at about 700° C.

Ice glass
Thus named because of its resemblance to the surface of ice. It is obtained by immersing the semi-worked piece when still hot in cold water then returning it to the furnace.

Incalmo
Technique consisting of joining separately worked pieces by heating that will make up a single object.

Levada
Operation of taking the melted glass from the pot with the blowpipe.

Manaretta or Maneretta
Tool similar to a comb, used to make surface decorations such as festoons.

Marble
Roll the glass on an iron plate, once in bronze or marble, to give the glass taken from the pot the desired shape.

Mezza stampaura
Decorative technique, previously used on Roman glass and revived in Murano, consisting of placing the base of a blown object, still attached to the blowpipe, in a vitreous half mould that has been

imprinted in an open mould with negative ribbing that will become positive in the object.

MORISE
Decoration obtained with vitreous threads in a contrasting colour applied hot to a piece of glass and pinched with *borselle da pissegar* pincers.

MOSAIC GLASS
Glass made with sections of cane of different colour and design, cast together by heating.

MILK GLASS
Opaque, white glass, of a similar colour to milk, from which it gets its name, imitating porcelain.

PHOENICIAN GLASS
Thus named because it was an imitation of pre-Roman glass with a crumbly core, obtained by wrapping vitreous threads around a friable core that was subsequently eliminated. In Murano it was blown and decorated with vitreous filaments shaped with the *maneretta.*

PONTELLO
Solid iron rod with which the glass is supported when it is being worked in the part originally attached to the blowpipe.

POT
Recipient of different sizes in highly refractory material placed inside the furnace and used to cast the vitrescible mixture. Also called *padella.*

PULEGOSO GLASS
Opaque glass with a rough surface due to the inclusion of air bubbles (*puleghe*).

SPEO
Small, solid iron rod used to take small quantities of glass from the pot for decorations.

SUBMERGED GLASS
Glass that is made up of several transparent, differently coloured layers. It is made by immersing the glass being worked in pots containing molten glass of various colours.

SUPIETO
Hollow iron shaft that ends with a cone into which the master blows to unify the thickness of the glass.

TAGIANTI
Scissors of various shape used to cut the excess molten or only partially cooled glass.

VITRESCIBLE MIXTURE
Mix of various raw materials carefully weighed and mixed, ready to be put into the pot and cast.

WHEEL ENGRAVING
Decorative technique with which various patterns are marked on the surface of the glass with incisions of varying depth, using copper discs covered with an abrasive material. Also called *rotella* or *rotina* engraving.

Bibliography

Prima Esposizione vetraria muranese inaugurata nel 1864, Venice 1864

V. Zanetti, *Guida di Murano e delle celebri sue fornaci vetrarie*, Venice 1866

Sulla Seconda Esposizione vetraria del 1869 in Murano. Discorsi, notizie e relazioni, Venice 1869

B. Cecchetti, V. Zanetti, E. Sanfermo, *Monografia della Vetraria veneziana e muranese*, Venice 1874

R. Santini, *Ricordo della III Esposizione vetraria di Murano, 1895, Versi con note illustrative*, Venice 1895

R. Gallo, *Giuseppe Briati e l'arte del vetro a Murano nel XVIII secolo*, Venice 1953

A. Gasparetto, *Il vetro di Murano dalle origini a oggi*, Venice 1958

G. Boesen, *Venetianske glas pä Rosenborg*, København 1960

A. Gasparetto, *Vetri di Murano 1860-1960*, exhibition catalogue (Verona, Palazzo della Gran Guardia), Verona 1960

G. Mariacher, *Il vetro soffiato*, Milan 1960

G. Mariacher, *Vetri italiani del Rinascimento*, Milan 1963

G. Mariacher, *Vetri graffiti veneziani del '500*, Venice s. d.

R. Barovier Mentasti, *Vetri di Murano del '900*, exhibition catalogue (Murano, Museo Vetrario), Milan 1977

R. Barovier Mentasti, *Vetri di Murano dell'800*, exhibition catalogue (Murano, Museo Vetrario), Milan 1978

A. Dorigato, *Vetri di Murano del '700*, exhibition catalogue (Murano, Museo Vetrario), Milan 1981

R. Barovier Mentasti, *Il vetro veneziano*, Milan 1982

R. Barovier Mentasti, A. Dorigato, A. Gasparetto, T. Toninato (edited by), *Mille anni di arte del vetro a Venezia*, exhibition catalogue (Venice, Palazzo Ducale and Museo Correr), Venice 1982

A. Dorigato, *Murano, il vetro a tavola ieri e oggi*, exhibition catalogue (Murano, Museo Vetrario), Venice 1983

A. Dorigato, *Vetri*, in F. Dal Co, G. Mazzariol (edited by), *Carlo Scarpa 1906-1978*, exhibition catalogue (Venice, Gallerie dell'Accademia), Milan 1984

A. Dorigato, *Vetri del Settecento e dell'Ottocento*, Novara 1985

A. Dorigato, *Vetri. Rinascimento e Barocco*, Novara 1985

A. Dorigato, *Il vetro-mosaico muranese*, in 'Bollettino dei Civici Musei Veneziani d'Arte e di Storia', XXIX, n.s., 1985

A. Dorigato, *Il Museo Vetrario di Murano*, Milan 1986

A. Dorigato, *Guido Balsamo Stella designer di vetri*, in *Guido Balsamo Stella 1882-1941*, exhibition catalogue (Bassano del Grappa, Palazzo Agostinelli), Bassano del Grappa 1987

A. Dorigato, *Il vetro soffiato di Murano alle esposizioni di Ca' Pesaro*, in *Venezia. Gli anni di Ca' Pesaro, 1908-1920*, exhibition catalogue (Venice, Ca' Pesaro), Milan 1987

L. Zecchin, *Vetro e vetrai di Murano. Studi sulla storia del vetro*, vol. I, Venice 1987 (printed on the initiative of the Associazione per la Storia e lo Sviluppo della Cultura muranese)

L. Zecchin, *Vetro e vetrai di Murano. Studi sulla storia del vetro*, vol. II, Venice 1989 (printed on the initiative of the Associazione per la Storia e lo Sviluppo della Cultura muranese)

Salviati, il suo vetro e i suoi uomini, 1859-1987, Venice 1989

G. Sarpellon, *Miniature di vetro. Murrine 1838-1924*, Venice 1990

L. Zecchin, *Vetro e vetrai di Murano. Studi sulla storia del vetro*, vol. III, Venice 1990 (printed on the initiative of the Associazione per la Storia e lo Sviluppo della Cultura muranese)

M. Barovier (edited by), *Napoleone Martinuzzi vetraio del Novecento*, exhibition catalogue (Venice, Galleria Marina Barovier), Venice 1992

M. Quesada, *Hans St. Lerche: uno scultore norvegese tra Roma e Murano*, in *L'arte del vetro. Silice e fuoco: vetri del XIX e XX secolo*, exhibition catalogue (Rome, Palazzo delle Esposizioni), Venice 1992

Umberto Bellotto 1882-1940. Ricami in ferro e vetro, exhibition catalogue (Milan, Galleria Balzaretti), Milan 1992

R. Barovier Mentasti, *Vetri veneziani del '900. La collezione della Cassa di Risparmio di Venezia - Biennali 1930-1970*, Venice 1993

Gli Artisti di Venini. Per una storia del vetro d'arte veneziano, exhibition catalogue (Venice, Fondazione Giorgio Cini), Milan 1996

M. Barovier, *Carlo Scarpa, i vetri di un architetto*, exhibition catalogue (Brescia, Palazzo Martinengo), Milan 1997

A. Bova, R. Junck, P. Migliaccio (edited by), *I bicchieri di Murano dell'800*, exhibition catalogue (Venice, Galleria Rossella Junck), Venice 1998

A. Dorigato (edited by), *Vetri veneziani: Ohira*, exhibition catalogue (Venice, Museo Correr), Venice 1998

A. Dorigato, *Il vetro a murrine e gli artisti del '900*, in A. Bova, R. Junck, P. Migliaccio (edited by), *Murrine e millefiori nel vetro di Murano dal 1830 al 1930*, exhibition catalogue (Venice, Fondazione Querini Stampalia), Venice 1998

R. Junck, *La produzione della Fratelli Toso dal 1854 alla prima guerra mondiale*, in A. Bova, R. Junck, P. Migliaccio (edited by), *Murrine e millefiori nel vetro di Murano dal 1830 al 1930*, exhibition catalogue (Venice, Fondazione Querini Stampalia), Venice 1998

A. Dorigato (edited by), *Avventurine. Massimo Nordio*, exhibition catalogue (Venice, Museo Correr), Venice 1999

Michele Burato, Isabelle Poilprez, Andrea Zilio, exhibition catalogue (Venice, Galleria Rossella Junck), Venice 1999

R. Barovier Mentasti, *La vetreria Venini tra Murano e Milano*, in A. Venini Diaz de Santillana, *Venini: catalogo ragionato 1921-1986*, Milan 2000

A. Dorigato (edited by), *Strano ma vetro. Maria Grazia Rosin*, exhibition catalogue (Venice, Museo Correr), Milan 2000

A. Venini Diaz de Santillana, *Venini: catalogo ragionato 1921-1986*, Milan 2000

A. Dorigato, *L'arte del vetro a Murano*, San Giovanni Lupatoto 2002

Photolithography
Fotolito Veneta, San Martino Buonalbergo (Verona)

Printed by
Grafiche Nardin, Ca' Savio - Cavallino - Treporti
(Venice)
for Marsilio Editori® s.p.a. in Venice

EDITION	YEAR
10 9 8 7 6 5 4 3 2 1	2006 2007 2008 2009 2010